THE NAUTILUS
ADVANCED
BODYBUILDING
BOOK

W9-CFQ-976

THE NAUTILUS
ADVANCED
BODYBUILDING
BOOK

BY ELLINGTON DARDEN, PH.D.

FIRESIDE

A Fireside Book
Published by Simon & Schuster, Inc.
New York

Also by Ellington Darden

The Superfitness Handbook

The Nautilus Book: An Illustrated Guide to Physical Fitness the Nautilus Way

Strength-Training Principles

The Athlete's Guide to Sports Medicine

The Nautilus Nutrition Book

The Darden Technique for Weight Loss, Body Shaping and Slenderizing

The Nautilus Woman

No More Fat!

The Nautilus Bodybuilding Book

ACKNOWLEDGMENTS

I would like to recognize and thank the following people who contributed to *The Nautilus Advanced Bodybuilding Book*.

Chris Lund, photographer, for imparting an "in-the-gym feel" to the pictures throughout the book.

Boyer Coe, Mr. America, Mr. World, and Mr. Universe and currently a professional bodybuilding champion, for demonstrating the advanced routines and for making useful suggestions throughout.

Mike Mentzer, Mr. America and Mr. Universe, and Ray Mentzer, Mr. America, for reading portions of the manuscript and offering valuable comments.

Julie McNew, women's bodybuilding champion, for demonstrating the exercises in Chapter 19.

Vic Tanny, Sr., for the hours he spent talking to me about the California bodybuilding scene during the 1940s.

Arthur Jones, creator, developer, and driving force behind Nautilus, for making it all possible.

The photography in this book, except as noted, was done by Chris Lund.

Important Note

Bodybuilders who train on Nautilus equipment in commercial fitness centers should have the management's approval before trying any workout in this book. Under some circumstances, it may not be practical or advisable to perform certain advanced routines.

Copyright © 1984 by Ellington Darden, Ph.D.
All rights reserved
including the right of reproduction in whole or in part in any form
A Fireside Book
Published by Simon & Schuster, Inc.
Simon & Schuster Building, Rockefeller Center
1230 Avenue of the Americas, New York, New York 10020
FIRESIDE and colophon are registered trademarks of Simon & Schuster, Inc.
Designed by Martin Moskof Associates, Inc.
Manufactured in the United States of America
Printed and bound by The Murray Printing Company
3 4 5 6 7 8 9 10
ISBN: 0-671-49246-2

CONTENTS

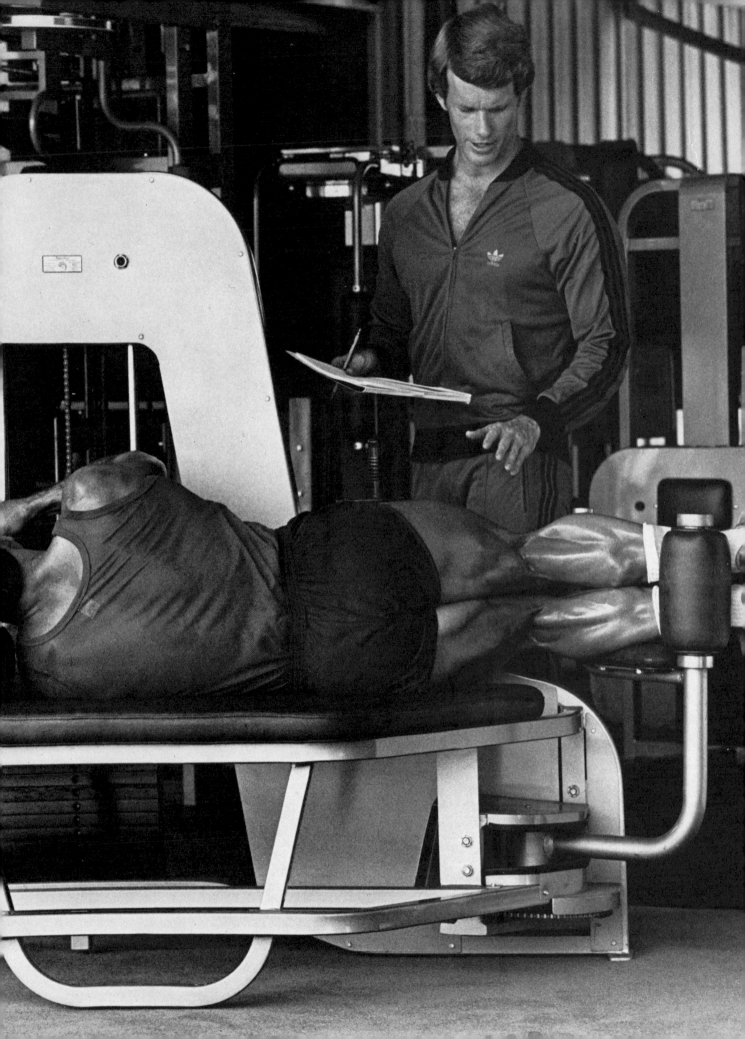

PREFACE

T o get maximum results from *The Nautilus Advanced Bodybuilding Book*, it is essential to familiarize yourself with Nautilus concepts and equipment. If you haven't read *The Nautilus Bodybuilding Book*, published in 1982, you'd be wise to do so. It provides you with a clear understanding of the science of Nautilus training.

Please be forewarned: The new routines described in this advanced book are not for beginners. They are for bodybuilders who have trained seriously for at least one year.

If you are not a dedicated bodybuilder, put down this book immediately. Forget it. It's not for you.

The routines require 100 percent concentration and 100 percent intensity of effort. Unless you're willing to put forth such dedication, then don't bother.

The first section, Advanced Considerations, comprises ten chapters. Most of this material is based on the writings of Arthur Jones, the inventor of Nautilus equipment and the president of Nautilus Sports/Medical Industries. These chapters provide you with a deeper understanding of Nautilus bodybuilding principles.

The second section, Advanced Routines, furnishes you with specific Nautilus workouts to build massive muscles efficiently. "Why spend years building your body," asks Arthur Jones, "when you could do the same thing in months?"

If you're serious about bodybuilding, if you can follow directions, if you're not afraid of hard work, and if you want maximum muscular growth in minimum time, *The Nautilus Advanced Bodybuilding Book* is for you.

Ellington Darden, Ph.D.
Lake Helen, Florida

Ellington Darden training Boyer Coe on the Nautilus side leg curl machine.

PART ONE

ADVANCED CONSIDERATIONS

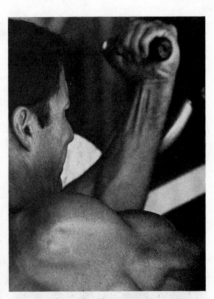

CHAPTER 1
NAUTILUS
BUILDS MUSCLE
FAST

Nautilus builds muscle, and it builds muscle fast.

Ray Mentzer, on his first visit to Nautilus Sports/Medical Industries, weighed 253 pounds. He was in fair condition, with an upper arm measuring 19¾ inches. During his brief visit, he requested a supervised workout from Arthur Jones. The date was January 5, 1983.

Jones started Ray on the duo squat machine. The weight was set at 385 pounds and the seat adjusted until the cams were fully unwound when Ray's legs were straight.

Ray began performing the repetitions slowly and smoothly in an alternating fashion. After 8 repetitions with each leg, Ray was breathing like a freight train. But he continued at his deliberate pace.

And Jones continued spurring him on in his commanding voice: "That's it, Ray. Keep going. Stay with it." Ray failed with his left leg on the 16th repetition.

Jones reduced the weight on the duo squat to 310 pounds. Ray gritted his teeth and went back to work. He found the going tougher than expected as he huffed and puffed his way through 6 more repetitions with each leg.

His face showed his inner dismay. He'd bought it for the day. "Damn, that's all I can do," he complained to Jones.

"The hell you say," Arthur Jones growled at him. "You came here to work, and you will by God *work*. Get ready." Jones was measuring every detail, and it was important that Mentzer continue in the akinetic-infimetric manner.

With 85 pounds on the machine and the movement-restraining bar in place, Ray worked one leg against the other infimetrically for another 30 seconds.

Suddenly Ray's face contorted in pain. A scream burst from him as he rolled from the machine and collapsed on the floor. His legs resembled two great vibrating machines twitching in unison. You could actually see the blood pumping furiously to them.

Jones waited precisely one minute and then gestured to his assistants. "Help him to his feet," he ordered. The men pulled Ray from the floor, his face still twisted in a grimace. They measured his pulse rate at an astonishing 204 beats per minute—60 seconds *after* he'd finished the movement.

Ray's physiological changes were astonishing. His thighs were still pumped to such dimensions he couldn't remove his sweatpants. They were squeezed tightly against his legs. Jones made a conservative estimate that Ray's thighs had expanded by at least 2 inches.

"Rest quietly for a few more minutes," Jones told Mentzer. Ray took the offer like a whipped dog given a reprieve. It didn't last long. Jones checked the time and nodded again to Ray. "Up. Let's go," he said impatiently.

Jones pushed Mentzer through seven additional exercises: lower back, chin, dip, pullover, pulldown, arm cross, and decline press. When he completed his work on the final machine, we again measured Ray's pulse rate. It read 190 beats per minute! Clearly, his heart, lungs, and muscles had sustained tremendous stress for the duration of the workout.

"Dammit, Arthur, you're killing me," Ray agonized.

Jones ignored the complaint. "Try this program for the next several months," he challenged Mentzer. "You do one set to failure of eight exercises, repeated *only* twice a week. Got it? And I guarantee your body will respond. Cut your calories slightly to eliminate your excess body fat." He studied the still-pained Mentzer. "Okay?" Jones prodded.

"Okay, okay," Ray answered through gritted teeth. "I won't like it, but . . ."

The 20⅜-inch arm of Ray Mentzer. *(Photo by Ellington Darden)*

"No one asked you to like it," Jones threw at him, gesturing to Mentzer to hit the showers. Ray looked like a huge kid who'd lost a street fight as he turned the corner for the showers. Arthur Jones grinned. Mentzer had taken the challenge and he would prove Jones's arguments.

Ray flew back to California, continued his workouts as he had been instructed to do, and returned to Florida on February 21, 1983. He looked —well, incredible. He had gained 7 pounds, but he was far leaner than the last time we'd seen him. Leaner and meaner as far as conditioning was concerned.

Arthur studied him carefully. "You stick with that program?" The question was rhetorical. He wanted Ray's *attitude* more than his confirmation.

Ray nodded. "Like clockwork. Just like you told me," he said. "Twice a week every week for six weeks." His face brightened. "You know what? I've had to alter my pants twice. The thighs had to be made larger and the waist smaller. I can hardly believe it. But I can now handle the entire weight stack on the duo squat machine."

Arthur Jones showed only a poker face. He gestured impatiently. "Let's see what your arm measures."

Ray rolled up his sleeve and contracted his biceps. Arthur made the measurements, and we saw the first indication of pleasure. "Now, pay attention," he commanded Ray and the others. "This shows what serious, no-nonsense training can produce. It's 20⅛ inches. That's ⅜ inch more than it was previously. And it looks like you've added at least 15 pounds of muscle to your body as well.

"Let me tell you something, Ray. You've got the potential to be the biggest bodybuilder the world has ever seen. But . . ." Arthur paused for several seconds, raised his craggy eyebrows, and looked directly at Ray, "the key to reaching your potential is figuring out ways to make your training harder, but briefer."

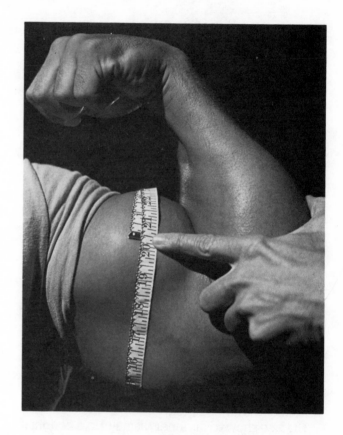

On July 9, 1983, Ray Mentzer's cold upper arm measured 20⅜ inches.

Harder, But Briefer

Ray Mentzer demonstrated to himself in six weeks that Nautilus training was more productive than any other type of exercise.

But why?

Because Nautilus is harder than any other type of exercise; the intensity of effort is greater. Or, at least, it should be.

Running will produce more muscular growth than walking, simply and only because the intensity of effort involved in running is greater than it is in walking.

But it should also be noted that you can stand almost any amount of walking, but that you cannot stand nearly as much running.

And the faster you run, the less running you can stand.

There are two basic factors in muscle-building exercise. One is good, the other is bad.

Intensity of effort is good. Anything that increases the intensity of an exercise will improve it.

Amount of exercise is bad. It is the amount of exercise that exhausts your recovery ability and makes growth impossible, or even produces losses in size and strength.

While it is true that you can stand a great amount of exercise if the intensity is low, it is also true that such exercise will never produce much in the way of worthwhile results.

And it is equally true that you cannot stand much exercise if the intensity is high.

Thus, the intensity must be high in order to stimulate growth, and the amount of exercise must be very little in order to permit growth. It follows that you should train very hard, and very briefly.

A Practical Example

At a rate of 2 miles per hour, you can walk a distance of 20 miles without even getting tired. Doing so, however, will do little to promote muscular growth.

But if you double the intensity by increasing your speed to 4 miles per hour, then you will find that even 4 miles of walking becomes harder than 20 miles at the lower speed.

Thus it should be obvious that doubling the intensity requires you to reduce the amount by about 80 percent.

And if you step up the speed to 8 miles per hour, then it is likely that 1 mile will be about all you want.

Again, raising the intensity requires a lowering of the amount. If you raise the intensity a little, then you must reduce the amount by a lot.

Insofar as its effect on the recovery ability is concerned, there is a geometrical relationship involved in exercise. If you double the intensity, you cannot compensate by cutting the amount in half. Instead, you must reduce the amount of exercise greatly in order to permit a small increase in intensity.

Muscle-Building Propaganda

Almost every one of the training schedules published in the muscle magazines during the last 30 years has been outright hogwash. The author urges the reader to train as hard as possible, and then lists a workout schedule that makes hard training impossible. So the enthusiastic trainees read this garbage. They look at the pictures of their hero—the supposed author—try to follow a similar routine, and end up with a case of nervous exhaustion, and no muscles.

So most of them quit in disgust, wrongly convinced that exercise is of no value, for them at least.

A few stick it out, with little to show for their efforts apart from a constantly dragged-out feeling and no energy for their other daily activities.

But a very few do show something in the way of results for their work—eventually. These few do finally manage to produce a degree of muscular size that should come from three or four months of proper exercise, but it takes them three or four years to do it.

But none of them do anything even closely related to workouts that they read about.

Simply because such workouts are impossible. Not difficult—outright impossible! Almost any one of the published workouts would kill Hercules himself.

And even if you could live through such a workout, it would not build muscle. Instead, it would produce muscular losses. You would quickly grow weaker instead of becoming stronger.

The few trainees who do stick it out usually make the same old mistake of equating *more* with *better.* And they are encouraged in such beliefs by what they read in muscle magazines. Since *training hard* and *training a lot* are mutually exclusive factors, the bodybuilder is literally forced to reduce the intensity of his workouts in order to continue training as much as he thinks he has to.

There is no choice in the matter. You cannot train hard and train a lot at the same time. Such is simply impossible.

Jones's Personal Experience

Arthur Jones learned that lesson very clearly more than 30 years ago. He is quick to admit, however, that it had to be forced on him by personal experience.

Having reached what he then considered the absolute top limit of his personal physical potential, he discovered by accident that the secret to greater growth was to train less.

When he reduced his workouts by exactly half, he suddenly found himself growing again—growing fast, quickly reaching a size and strength that he previously thought was impossible for his body.

Later, having reached a higher plateau or sticking point, he again reduced his workouts. This time he cut his total weekly training time to an

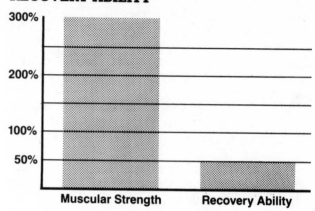

MUSCULAR STRENGTH AND RECOVERY ABILITY

The typical, untrained man has the potential to increase his strength by 300 percent before he reaches his full potential. But his recovery ability, the chemistry that is necessary for his body to overcompensate and get stronger, does not increase in proportion to his strength. His recovery ability increases only 50 percent. The stronger a man becomes, the greater demands he makes on his recovery ability. Thus, his body needs harder, but briefer, exercise for continued growth stimulation.

Arthur Jones explains to Boyer Coe that over 30 years of training experience have taught him that the secret of continued muscular growth is to train less. *(Photo by Ellington Darden)*

amount that he had previously used in each of three weekly workouts. As a result of training only a third as much as he did earlier, Jones quickly started growing again.

For Arthur Jones, that was the turning point that started his thinking on the path of a logical approach to exercise. The cause-and-effect relationship was now evident to Jones. As he became stronger, it was necessary to reduce the amount of training to produce continued progress. The stronger he became, the more strain he imposed on his recovery ability.

Most trainees, however, never seem to learn that lesson from their own experiences. Instead, as they grow stronger and impose greater loads on their recovery ability they gradually reduce the intensity of their workouts when they should be reducing the amount of training. Remember— you cannot have both. You can have intensity or a large amount of exercise, but not both.

Arthur Jones then started looking for ways to increase the intensity factor, the good factor, the productive factor, the growth-stimulating factor. Every time he did find a way to increase the intensity, he immediately encountered additional proof that another reduction in the amount of training was then required.

Nautilus Training

The development of Nautilus machines and Nautilus training was based on an awareness that it was desirable to increase the intensity of exercise. The proper use of Nautilus equipment has merely confirmed the fact that a great amount of training is not necessary.

Again there was really no choice in the matter. Since the Nautilus machines do raise the intensity of exercise to a level that is impossible to attain in any other manner, it was necessary to reduce the amount of training. At first we produced what we considered to be very good results by performing

Nautilus is constantly trying to make its machines more efficient. This is one of the prototype shops at Nautilus Sports/
Medical Industries in Lake Helen, Florida.

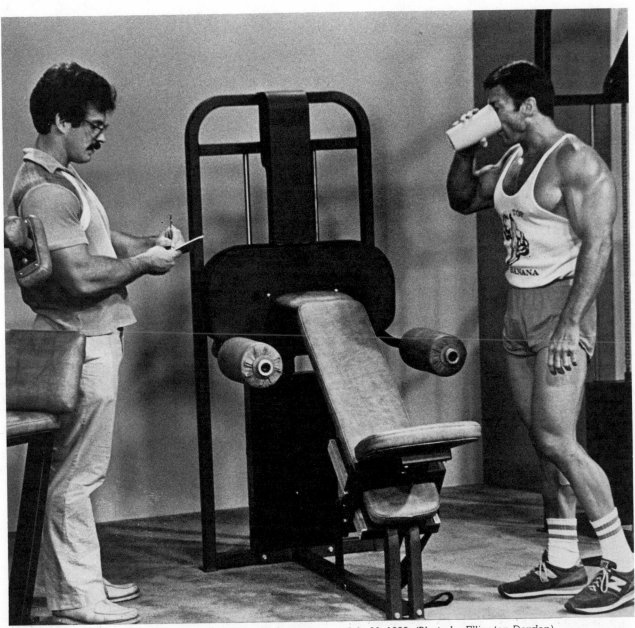

Mike Mentzer keeps records for Boyer Coe during his workout on July 20, 1983. *(Photo by Ellington Darden)*

only three sets. Then we found that we got even better results from only two sets. Now we seldom perform more than one set of each exercise in a workout, and our results are far better than they were previously.

Twice-a-Week Training

Most of our current bodybuilders are training only twice each week, and usually for less than 30 minutes during each workout. None of them is training more than three times weekly. It may well be true that some bodybuilders can stand more training than that—but we are beginning to believe that most bodybuilders will produce the best results from even less training.

Many bodybuilders will at first find the above facts hard to accept. This will be particularly true if they have been habitually training five or six days a week and for three to four hours during each workout. But in the meantime, many thousands of other trainees have already discovered that they can produce far better results from a small fraction of their previously practiced training schedules.

Ray Mentzer, for example, has tried various types of training schedules. He has done ten sets per body part, split routines, and as much as ten hours per week training. His most productive workouts, however, have been his one set to failure of a limited number of Nautilus exercises, which exercises are repeated only twice a week.

Below is an exercise-by-exercise listing of Ray's Nautilus workout on June 15, 1983. The numbers before the slash indicate the weight used, and the numbers after the slash indicate the repetitions. Ray's strength, you'll note, exceeded the selectorized weight available on most Nautilus machines. Therefore, he pinned additional resistance on the side of the weight stack.

1. Duo squat   560/20
2. Pullover   275/8
3. Behind-neck pulldown   200/9
4. Lateral raise   290/7
5. Overhead press   200/11
6. 10° chest   275/8
7. Multi biceps   190/10
8. Lower back   400/12

It is a safe bet that no bodybuilder today can duplicate the resistance and repetitions that Ray used in the above workout.

Women and Nautilus

Julie McNew, an elite bodybuilder on the women's circuit, trained on Nautilus equipment in Florida with Ray and Mike Mentzer during the spring and summer of 1983. She performed the same advanced routines as did Ray and Mike, but with less resistance. Chapter 19 describes Julie's arm and shoulder routine. Be sure to read it, because Julie's arms and shoulders are unique in women's bodybuilding.

Women have the same number of skeletal muscles as men. Muscular function, regardless of sex, is identical. Male and female muscle requirements for growth are the same. It is important to understand, however, that women do not have the same genetic potential for building muscular size and strength as men. The average man can increase his muscular strength by 300 percent before he reaches his potential. The average woman can increase her muscular strength by approximately 150 percent before she reaches hers.

Ray Mentzer and Julie McNew are not your average man and woman. Both have unusual physiques: primarily long muscle bellies and short tendons. As a result, they have excellent potential for building muscular size and strength.

It is interesting to compare Julie's best performances to Ray's in the same Nautilus workout. Julie's height is 5 feet 4 inches, and she weighed 124½ pounds when she performed the following:

1. Duo squat   285/22

Ray Mentzer on the Nautilus overhead press machine. *(Photo by Lewis Green)*

2.	Pullover (women's)	170/11
3.	Behind-neck pulldown	100/11
4.	Lateral raise	100/6
5.	Overhead press	110/6
6.	10° chest	100/11
7.	Multi biceps	70/7
8.	Lower back	150/13

Julie's average strength on seven Nautilus machines (the men's and women's pullover are not comparable) is approximately 43 percent of Ray's. But remember, Julie weighs half as much as Ray.

The Nautilus harder, briefer training works for Ray Mentzer. It works for Julie McNew. Properly organized and properly applied, it will work for you.

Less Is Best

During the last 30 years, a large number of bodybuilders seem to have devoted most of their attention to determining how much exercise they can stand. At Nautilus, we are trying to determine how little exercise is actually required to get the biggest possible muscles. And while an exact answer is not yet available for every trainee, a general answer is obvious: *very little*. Very little, at least, if it is Nautilus exercise.

Julie McNew pushes for one more repetition on the Nautilus overhead press machine. *(Photo by Ellington Darden)*

Nautilus training works for Julie McNew. *(Photo by Ellington Darden)*

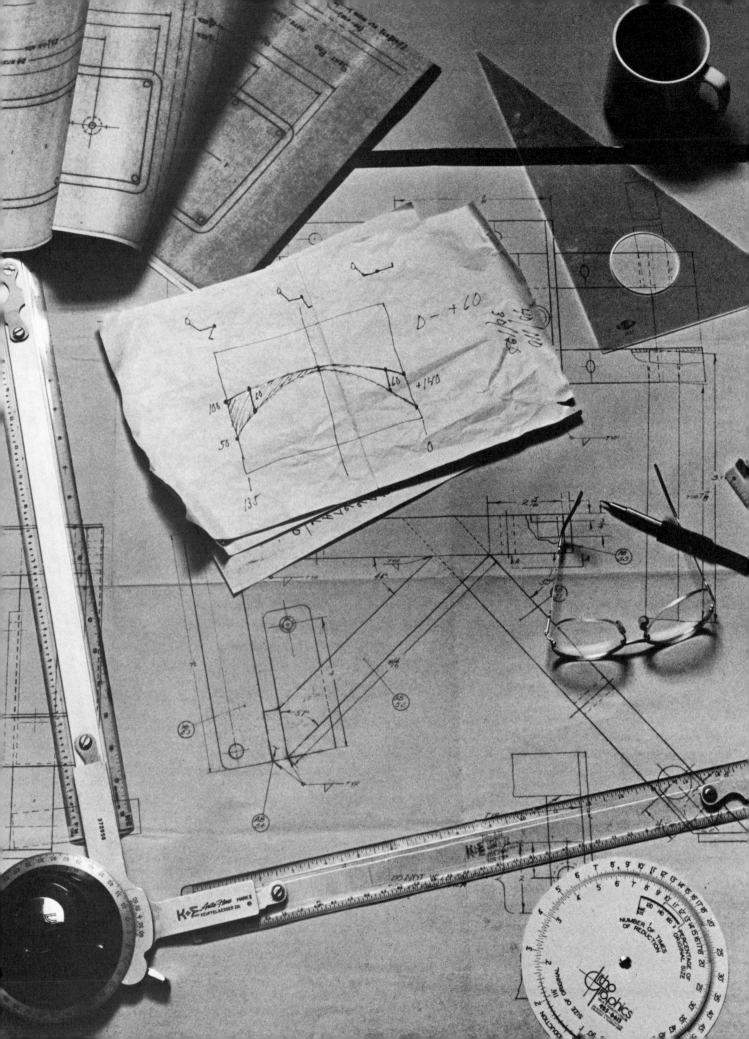

CHAPTER 2
SOME OF
THE PROBLEMS—
AND A FEW ANSWERS

Before you can begin a logical search for an answer, you must first understand the problem. And even if you are merely seeking practical results and have little interest in why such results are produced, you still must be aware of the cause-and-effect relationships involved.

Yet for the average person, too much theory is sometimes worse than none—since it frequently produces more confusion than practical knowledge. But you must, at least, know what to do and what results to expect.

The Relationship Between the Biceps and the Thumb

The average bodybuilder, for example, is seldom aware that a relationship exists between the biceps muscle of the upper arm and the thumb at the end of the same arm. Yet the function of the biceps dictates both the location and the function of the thumb. Without a thumb, the prime function of the biceps would be almost useless. Or if the thumb were located at the bottom of the hand instead of the top, then the function of the biceps would again be almost useless.

The thumb serves as an anchor for the hand during twisting movements. When the right hand is twisted in a clockwise fashion, the grip of the fingers would be torn loose if the hand was not anchored by the thumb. The bottom of the hand requires no anchor, since the direction of force application presses that part of the hand firmly against the object being gripped. Thus two thumbs, one at the top and another at the bottom of the hand, are not required.

For twisting in an opposite direction, another arm is provided—a mirror-image arm instead of a duplicate. Two right arms (instead of a right and a left) would merely provide unrequired duplication—and make it impossible to exert much in the way of twisting force in a counterclockwise

direction.

Why was the above example used? And just where is this discussion leading?

The example was selected because it relates to a muscle that attracts the attention of most bodybuilders, but that few trainees really understand. If you do understand the relationship between the biceps and the thumb, then it becomes possible to apply that knowledge to your training. Without such an understanding, your biceps training will probably be hit or miss at best.

"But," you may be tempted to say, "lots of bodybuilders have managed to produce outstanding biceps muscles and they have done so with little understanding of the facts."

Perfectly true, but how long did it take them? And it's worth mentioning that for each bodybuilder who did manage to produce outstanding biceps, there are at least a thousand with only average biceps.

The primary function of the biceps of the right arm is twisting the hand in a clockwise direction. And for proper exercise, the biceps must be worked against twisting resistance. Regardless of how much exercise you provide for the bending function of the biceps, you are *not* working the biceps completely. You are working only part of the muscle, and the least important part at that.

But even if you do provide exercise only for the bending function, the biceps will grow. It will grow as a result of indirect effect, the same result that is produced when your arms grow as a result of exercise for your legs. But it will grow slowly, and it will not grow as much as it would if it were exposed to proper exercise.

Training Right Means Training Less

You can produce results even if you train wrong. But you can produce much better results if you train right. And please note that the results you produce by training wrong will frequently be

Nautilus machines are scientifically designed according to the primary functions of human muscles. (*Photo by Lewis Green*)

The superbly peaked biceps of Arnold Schwarzenegger. *(Photo by Inge Cook)*

losses instead of gains.

The simple truth is that almost all of the training effort being expended by millions of bodybuilders produces exactly the opposite result from that desired. Most training actually prevents growth rather than promotes it.

That is not meant to imply that you should not train at all. You certainly should train—but you should train right, and you should not train too much. Training right isn't easy, but it is very easy to train too much.

There is a natural inclination to equate more with better. In the field of exercise, that is a terrible mistake.

Every time you hit a nail with a hammer you should drive it deeper into the wood. Every time you train you should stimulate growth. But it is very easy to hit a nail wrong and bend it, thus making it almost impossible to drive it properly. It is even easier to train wrong, making growth impossible, or producing positive results at only a snail's pace.

There is a definite limit to the muscular size and strength that you can produce, and this limit is determined entirely by heredity. The limits for some people are much lower than the limits for other people. But be assured that nobody has yet reached the limits of his or her personal, individual potential. In other words, it should be stated that even Sergio Oliva and Arnold Schwarzenegger have not reached the limits of their muscular size.

But reaching such limits of individual potential does not involve training more. On the contrary, most bodybuilders fail at a point far below their potential as a result of too much training. Actually, the larger you get, the less you should train.

Getting Better Results with Fewer Exercises

The most productive barbell exercises are the basic movements: squats, standing presses, deadlifts, pullovers, and curls. But these are also the *hardest* exercises—and for that very reason, many trainees avoid them. They substitute endless sets of lighter, easier exercises and then wonder why their progress is slow or nonexistent.

If you are using the right exercises, and if you are training properly, then you don't need to train very much in order to produce good results. In fact, if you are training as hard as you should be, then you can't stand very much training. And remember, the stronger you get, the less training you can stand.

If you have been training with barbells for several years, and if you have recently encountered a period of little or no progress, then do yourself a favor and try the following program for a brief period.

First, stop training entirely for a full week. Give your system a chance to recover from its overtrained condition. Then start back with three weekly workouts of only 12 sets each—that's right, not 12 sets of each exercise, but a total of only 12 sets in each workout. Two sets of each of the following basic movements: squats, standing presses, chins, bench presses, standing barbell curls, and parallel dips. Perform the exercises in that order. Use an amount of weight that will permit approximately 8 repetitions in good form, and increase the weight as soon as you can perform 12 or more repetitions without cheating. Concentrate on the performance of strict, full-range movements.

Three weeks on such a program should produce growth at a rate that will probably shock you. When your rate of growth slows down, then reduce your program to a schedule of only two such weekly workouts.

Nowhere near enough? Don't knock it until you've tried it!

Not hard enough? It should be—and it will be if you use as much weight as you can, and if you

perform all of the exercises in perfect form and carry each set to a point of failure.

Putting Theory into Machines

The theory behind the above training program is simple. Such basic movements will stimulate growth in all of the major muscular structures of the body, and the brief amount of training will not exhaust your system to the point that growth is impossible.

The development of the Nautilus system of training was based upon a clear awareness that best results are always produced by practicing a few basic but hard exercises. We were not looking for an easy method of training—no such method that is productive will ever be found. Instead, we were looking for the hardest exercises that could be developed—and we found them.

So right from the start, Arthur Jones realized that the barbell is designed to make it easy to lift weights. Demonstrating strength is one thing, but building strength is a different matter. A barbell is probably the ideal tool for demonstrating strength, simply because a barbell makes it easy to lift a lot of weight. But a barbell certainly is not the best tool for building strength, for the same reason.

Obviously, then, we first had to determine and understand fully the problems encountered in barbell training. Secondly, we had to understand the requirements of muscles.

When we compared the functions of a muscle to the functions of a barbell it was immediately apparent that we were faced with more differences than similarities. For example, the function of a muscle produces rotary movement of the involved body part. The function of the triceps muscle causes the forearm to rotate around the axis of the elbow. Yet a barbell does not provide rotary resistance against this movement. Instead, a barbell provides straight-line resistance, resistance

The bench press can be made much more productive if it is performed slowly and smoothly without bouncing, and continued until momentary muscular failure.

produced by gravity.

The result being that the movement produced by the function of the triceps muscle is not provided with full-range resistance when you are training with a barbell. A barbell provides resistance for only part of the movement, involves only part of the mass of the triceps muscles—and the least important part, at that. If you perform four sets—or 40 sets—you are not working more of the triceps muscles. Instead, you are working the same part of the muscles repeatedly. The largest part of the muscles is not working at all.

So we had to design an exercise that would involve all of the mass of the triceps muscles. The only type of exercise that could involve all of the triceps muscles (or all of any muscle) is an exercise that provides rotary resistance.

Then, step by step, over a period of many years, we examined the functions and the requirements of all of the major muscular structures of the body. And, eventually, we understood the functions and knew what the requirements were. For a perfect form of exercise, the requirements are rotary-form, omnidirectional, double-direct, automatically variable, full-range, balanced resistance.

Total Resistance

When all of these requirements are provided, then it is impossible to move without encountering resistance. There is resistance at the start of a movement, resistance at the end of a movement, and resistance at every point during a movement. There are no sticking points where the resistance is too high, and there are no points during the movement where no resistance is encountered. Thus it is impossible to lock out under the weight, at least on the Nautilus rotary machines.

If you move, you are moving against resistance. If you stop, you are forced to hold that position against resistance. If you lower the weight, you are still working negatively against resistance.

Sergio Oliva performs a repetition on one of the first Nautilus pullover machines. The pullover provides over 240 degrees of rotary, direct resistance for the latissimus dorsi muscles. Note the thickness of Sergio's upper body. *(Photos by Inge Cook)*

We do not claim to be the only ones who realized the failings and shortcomings of barbell training. But it does appear that nobody else really understood the problems, and it is obvious that nobody else has done much in the way of solving the problems.

Understanding and Applying Practical Facts

At the start of this chapter, we mentioned the relationship of the thumb to the biceps. That example was used for a good reason. The thumb and the biceps are both involved in the same system. They are parts of a very practical mechanism which could not function properly if a part were missing.

Stand an empty barbell bar on end and support it in a vertical position. Grip it with your right hand, near the center of the bar. Now try to twist it to the right, in a clockwise direction. You will see that the thumb serves as a very effective anchor for the hand during such a twisting movement. But you might not be aware that the biceps of your right arm provides most of the power for that twisting movement. Without the thumb, you would not be able to make much practical use of the biceps.

Now try to twist in the opposite direction, to the left, in a counterclockwise direction. It will be obvious that you have much less strength for movements in that direction. And it will be equially obvious that the lack of a second thumb on the bottom of your hand makes it impossible to exert much force in that direction in any case. Because when twisting to the left with the right hand, the hand will be torn loose from its grip if much force is exerted—since there is no thumb on the bottom of the hand to serve as an anchor for such a direction of movement.

The Easy-Curl Bar

The relationship between the thumb and the

The easy-curl bar actually works against the biceps. The grip twists the hands in the wrong direction.

Rachel McLish works her biceps on the Nautilus omni biceps machine. Notice that her hands are supinated.

biceps should be clear and obvious, once you are aware of it. Yet, in fact, until Arthur Jones described that relationship nobody seemed even to notice such a simple point. Instead, the manufacturers of exercise devices devoted their attentions to designing gadgets that actually prevented the biceps from functioning in the only manner in which it can function properly. The so-called "easy-curl bar" is a prime example. Instead of improving the curl, it almost ruins it. The easy-curl bar certainly twists the grip, but it twists it in the wrong direction, forcing the biceps into a position where it cannot fully contract. In order to contract, a muscle must produce movement of the related body part. The easy-curl bar prevents such movement.

Palms Up or Palms Down?

Ask yourself a simple question: "Can I curl more with a palms-up grip or with a palms-down grip?" With a palms-up grip, of course. But why? Simply because, with a palms-up grip, your biceps muscles are twisted into a position where they can function properly. With a palms-down grip your biceps muscles are prevented from contracting fully and thus you are weaker.

For exactly the same reason, chinning movements to the chest should be performed with a palms-up grip. And chinning or pulldown movements to behind the neck should be performed with a parallel grip. The fully twisted or supinated grip places your biceps muscles into their strongest position. When the elbows are in front of your chest, as they are while you are performing a regular chinning movement, then a fully supinated grip will give you a palms-up grip. But when your elbows are back in line with your shoulders, as they are while you are performing a behind-the-neck chin or pulldown, then a fully supinated grip will produce a parallel grip, a grip where the palms are facing each other.

Yet, until Nautilus came along, millions of body-builders used the worst possible grip, a pronated grip. Their palms were twisted in the wrong direction, which forced their biceps into a position where it was difficult to produce much strength.

That might not have been bad if doing so had any worthwhile result. If, for example, using a pronated grip forced more work onto the latissimus muscles, then it might have been worthwhile. But, in fact, it merely served to make a bad problem worse. The problem was caused by weakness of the biceps in the first place—so making the biceps work in the weakest position merely made matters worse.

You fail in chinning and pulldown movements when the strength of the biceps is exhausted. This happens long before the larger and stronger latissimus muscles are close to a point of failure. So the biceps muscles get a fairly heavy workout from such exercises. But the muscles that you are really trying to work never get much more than a mild warm-up.

The Importance of Stretching in Maximum Contraction

Every physiologist should be aware of the fact that a muscle should be worked from a stretched position, that the starting position should be extreme to stimulate as many muscle fibers as possible.

And it should be obvious to anybody that such initial stretching is impossible without negative resistance—the back pressure that is required to move the involved body part into a stretched starting position.

That is another problem that is encountered in many barbell exercises. In the curl, for example, there is no initial stretch in spite of the fact that barbell exercises do provide negative resistance. And this is yet another advantage that Nautilus exercises have over barbell exercises—Nautilus

In the top half of preacher bench curling movements, the barbell travels horizontally rather than vertically. Little work is done by the biceps throughout the top position.

machines do provide stretch at the start of the movements.

In an attempt to get around the lack of stretch at the start of the curling movement with a barbell, somebody invented the "preacher curling bench." This bench certainly does provide the needed stretch at the start of the movement. But it does so at a terrible price! It removes resistance near the end of the movement, thus making it impossible to move anywhere near the fully contracted position while still encountering resistance.

Nautilus machines provide stretching at the start of the movement and also provide resistance at the end of the movement—and provide resistance throughout the movement.

The Nautilus Position

The simple fact is that Nautilus is in a very advantageous position. We are free to use, and we would use, anything that would improve the function of Nautilus machines. But we have chosen to restrict our attentions to the development of large, complex, heavy-duty machines. We have done so while being aware that we could greatly increase the sales of our machines by manufacturing less expensive types of equipment.

It simply is not possible to build a Rolls-Royce for the price of a wheelbarrow. So if you are limited to a wheelbarrow budget (as many people are), then train with an Olympic barbell.

If and when anything new comes on the scene that is an actual improvement, then it will be incorporated into the function of the Nautilus equipment. Furthermore, we will be the first to give full credit where any such credit is due. And even if any such new development *cannot* be incorporated into Nautilus equipment—for physical reasons, or legal reasons, or any other reasons—we will still be quick to give clear credit where credit is due.

CHAPTER 3
THE RELATIONSHIP
OF MUSCULAR
MASS AND STRENGTH

I ncreasing the size of a muscle will increase its strength, and the increase in strength will be in proportion to the increase in size. But it does not follow that a particular bodybuilder with larger muscles can always demonstrate more strength than another bodybuilder with smaller muscles.

The ability to demonstrate strength is determined by a number of factors, such as neurological efficiency, bodily proportions, skill, motivation, and muscular size. Thus, the size of the involved muscles is only a small factor, but an important one and the primary concern of this chapter.

Increasing the strength of a muscle by increasing its size is probably the most common goal in exercise. It is a goal that can be seen, measured, experienced. And it is a goal that can be reached quickly. Millions of people have devoted large parts of their lives to this goal, and thousands of books have been written on the subject. Yet the subject remains clouded by confusion.

The facts are simple enough, but separating the facts from the myths is not always so simple. One such myth concerns the relationship of muscular mass to strength.

Most of the confusion that forms the basis of the myths related to exercise results from the multiplicity of factors involved in producing, transmitting, and using muscular strength. A muscle produces strength, but it cannot transmit or use strength without the aid of other parts of the body.

Muscles, the Engines of the Body

In an automobile, the engine produces power. An engine is certainly required for the production of power, but is not of any practical use by itself. The power produced by the engine must be transmitted by the transmission and differential, and must be used by the wheels. A larger engine will produce more power, and if the other components of the power train are capable of withstand-

Samir Bannout, 1983 Mr. Olympia, has a winning blend of muscular mass and definition.

The strong, massive thighs of Tom Platz illustrate the relationship between muscular strength and muscular size.

ing the forces involved, then the increase in the size of the engine will produce an increase in the usable power of the automobile.

In the body, the muscles perform the functioning of a number of small engines, producing pulling forces in almost every direction. When the size of the muscles is increased, it becomes possible to produce more force. If that force is properly transmitted the result will be an increase in usable strength.

So increasing the size of an engine or a muscle will increase the available power. But an increase in size is not the only way to increase power. The power of an engine can also be increased by running it faster, and a similar result can be produced in a muscle. A muscle might be thought of as an engine with thousands of cylinders, but with only a rather small percentage of the cylinders attached to the electrical system at any one time. Only a few of the cylinders are available for the production of power at any given moment.

The production of power inside the cylinder of an engine is stimulated by an electrical spark. The contraction of a muscle fiber that produces power in the form of a pulling force is stimulated by an electrical impulse from the brain.

The speed, and thus the power, of an engine is limited by its ability to intake a proper fuel/air mixture. A muscle is limited in much the same way. If an electrical impulse from the brain reaches a particular muscle fiber that has exhausted its momentary supply of fuel and oxygen, then that fiber cannot contract. Since it is impossible for a muscle instantly to replace a depleted supply of fuel and oxygen, the resulting involvement of muscle fibers is on an alternating basis. Some fibers are working while other fibers are resting, replacing their stores of fuel and oxygen.

All of the fibers of a muscle are never working at any given instant, not even when the entire muscle is fresh.

Bertil Fox has an almost ideal combination of muscle mass and symmetry.

The Pace of Work

If the pace of work is slow enough to permit the resting fibers to replenish their stores of fuel and oxygen before the working fibers become exhausted, then the work can be continued for hours. Such work is called aerobic. Aerobic work will do little to increase the size or strength of the working muscles.

But if the pace of work is increased so that the working fibers become exhausted before the resting fibers have fully recuperated, then a point of muscular failure will eventually result.

The faster the pace of work, the faster a point of failure will be reached. This type, or pace, of work is called anaerobic. Anaerobic work is the type required for increasing the size and strength of muscles.

A widespread misunderstanding of the implications of the above point has resulted in very poor training practices. Increasing the pace of work does not require moving the resistance faster. On the contrary, exercises involving fast movement of the resistance will do little to increase strength.

The Importance of a Slow Speed of Movement

There is a definite limit to the possible speed of muscular contraction. If the speed of movement of the resistance is too fast, it literally outstrips the ability of the muscle to keep up. The result is that a large part of the muscle is not involved in the work at all. If a muscle is suddenly contracted while being exposed to a low level of resistance, very rapid movement of the resistance will occur. But only a small part of the muscle will be involved in the work. Movement will occur so fast that most of the muscle will never quite catch up; the movement will be completed before the muscle has time to contract.

Instead of increasing the pace of work by increasing the speed of movement, the resistance should be increased. If the resistance is heavy enough, sudden movement becomes impossible.

Sudden movement can also be produced in another manner, by throwing the weight. Throwing or heaving can be done in some cases where it would be impossible to move the resistance by contraction of the muscles that you are trying to exercise. Again, such exercise will do little in the way of increasing strength, the actual ability of a muscle to produce a pulling force.

But by involving a large number of other muscles in the movement, you probably will develop a style of performance that will enable you to "lift more weight" in a particular fashion. You may thus convince yourself and others that your strength has increased accordingly, when, in fact, your strength has probably remained unchanged.

For increasing muscular size and strength, movement should never be faster than the maximum speed of full-length muscular contraction. In practice, this means that the actual speed of movement should be quite slow. If you are capable of moving faster, then use more resistance. But do not increase the resistance to the point that it becomes necessary to throw the weight by involving other muscles.

Emphasizing Strict Form

A natural desire to show progress by increasing the resistance leads many bodybuilders into very poor training habits. True progress, as a result, comes to a halt or is produced very slowly. The resistance should be increased, and it should be increased as rapidly as possible. But it should not be increased by a sacrifice in the form.

A very strict style of performance is probably the single most important factor in exercise. It certainly is an absolute prerequisite for the production of outstanding bodybuilding results. Yet in practice, the style of performance of most bodybuilders varies from poor to pitiful.

The Importance of Full-Range Strength

When Boyer Coe first used the new Nautilus leg extension machine under Arthur Jones's supervision on March 2, 1983, he displayed a noticeable weakness in his quadriceps. This weakness was directly related to Boyer's habit of performing leg extensions by bouncing in and out of the contracted position. With 190 pounds on the machine, Boyer could smoothly move the resistance from the starting and midrange position. But he could not come to a complete stop in the fully contracted position. To get into the contracted position, he had to increase his speed of movement. As a result, he was unable to develop proportionate, full-range strength in the last 15 degrees of extension.

Jones had Coe reduce the resistance and concentrate on performing smooth, slow repetitions. Emphasis was placed on coming to a complete stop in the top position.

The technique worked. In three weeks, Boyer performed 11 perfect repetitions on the leg extension with 220 pounds. And on June 20, 1983, Boyer's quadriceps strength had improved to the extent that he did 310 pounds for 9 repetitions.

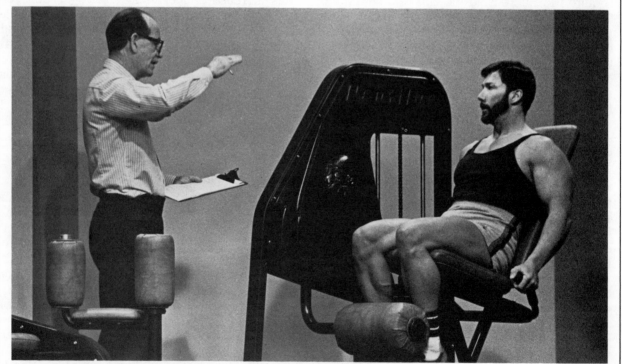

"If you want maximum muscular development of your quadriceps," Arthur Jones says to Boyer Coe, "you must come to a complete stop in the top position of the leg extension."

The resistance must be applied to the entire length of the muscles you are training. This is impossible if the movement is too fast, and also impossible if all or most of the work is actually performed by other muscles.

Comparing Strength

Most bodybuilders have seen examples of men who can lift a very heavy weight while showing little in the way of unusual muscular size, and other examples of men who cannot lift as much weight as you would expect from their muscular size. Such examples have caused numerous trainees to assume that muscular size has very little to do with strength. That impression, however, is exactly the opposite of the truth.

A short man may lift more weight than you would expect because he does not have to move it so far. The distance of movement is just as important as the actual amount of weight involved.

A lean, muscular man may lift more weight than a much larger man. But if all of the other factors are the same in both cases, then this is merely an indication that the smaller man actually has more muscular mass, and that the larger man's size is composed of a higher percentage of fatty tissue, which cannot produce force. Or a particular trainee may have developed a style of performance that permits him to move a heavy weight by throwing it. Thus he may appear to be stronger than another, larger trainee who is actually stronger.

In practice, it is almost impossible to compare fairly the strength of one man to that of another man. You can compare performances, but performance is not always a test of strength. Remember, strength is only one of several factors involved in any type of performance.

Size Equals Strength

In some ways the strength of a muscle can be compared to that of a rope, even though a rope cannot produce force by contraction. A rope can withstand a pulling force in proportion to its cross-sectional area. A muscle also can produce a pulling force in proportion to its cross-sectional area.

Since the length of a muscle is not changed by an increase in the volume of a muscle, it obviously follows that the cross-sectional area of a muscle is in direct proportion to the mass of a muscle. Thus the size of a muscle is a direct indication of the strength of the same muscle.

When you increase a particular man's muscular size, you will increase his strength. He will be stronger as a direct result of the increase in muscular size, and he will be stronger in proportion to the increase in muscular size. But he still may not be as strong as some other man with much smaller muscles. The smaller muscles of the other man may be working with advantages not available to the larger man.

In effect, any man will be stronger than he was if you increase the size of his muscles. But no one factor will ever make him equal to all other men.

Many of the other factors that contribute to demonstrations of strength cannot be changed, but you can increase the muscular size of almost anybody. Doing so will make any individual stronger than he was. *So the mass of a man's muscles is important for two reasons. One, it is directly related to his strength. Two, it is the factor most subject to change, the easiest factor to improve.*

A particular individual who has increased his muscular size as much as possible may still not be able to demonstrate as much strength as another man with less muscular mass. But he certainly will be able to demonstrate far more strength than he, as an individual, was capable of demonstrating before he increased his muscular size.

Bodybuilding or Weightlifting?

A large part of the confusion between muscular

In the 1960s in Cuba, Sergio Oliva was an excellent Olympic weightlifter. Sergio admits, however, that he was limited in his overhead lifting because of his broad shoulders and narrow waist. *(Photo by Inge Cook)*

size and strength undoubtedly results from current standards for physique competition. And at least part of this confusion also results from the fact that competitive weightlifters seldom have a bodybuilder type of physique.

A few bodybuilders are very strong. Most bodybuilders, however, cannot demonstrate a level of strength in proportion to their muscular size. Some bodybuilders, in fact, are actually quite weak when due consideration is given to their muscular mass. This weakness has absolutely nothing to do with the quality of their muscular mass. Their muscles, like those of anybody else, are strong in proportion to their size. But poor bodily leverage or some other factor makes it impossible for them to transmit a very high proportion of their muscular strength to their limbs. In effect, they have a powerful engine but a poor transmission. They can produce the power, but they can't use much of it.

Wide shoulders, narrow waist and hips, long legs, and short torso: given those bodily proportions and a greater than average muscular mass, and a man may become Mr. America. He may look strong, but in fact his strength cannot be in proportion to his appearance of strength. With those bodily proportions a man's muscles are forced to work at a grave disadvantage.

In contrast, a competitive weightlifter may not appear to have much more than an average amount of muscular mass, yet be able to demonstrate great strength. He almost certainly will have rather narrow shoulders, a thick waist and wide hips, short legs, and a long torso. Those are the bodily proportions required for building great strength. A man with those proportions, however, will seldom have a pleasing physique by present standards.

Over a period of the last 40 years, bodybuilders and weightlifters have gradually drifted apart, although they continued to use the same tool (the barbell), and usually performed much the same exercises. Men with the potential to build a Mr. America physique by present standards simply did not have the potential to demonstrate great strength. And men with the potential to build great strength could not produce the type of physique required for a Mr. America contest.

Usually within a short period of time after starting to train, an individual will almost be forced in one direction or the other. If his strength increases rapidly with little increase in his muscular mass, then he will be encouraged to turn his interests in the direction of competitive weightlifting. If his muscular mass increases out of proportion to his strength, then he will probably become a bodybuilder.

Draft horses are built for power. Racehorses are built for speed. And men fall into very similar categories. You can increase the muscular mass of a draft horse, and doing so will make him both stronger and faster, but it will never make him as fast as a good racehorse. And you can increase the muscular mass of a racehorse, and again it will make him both stronger and faster, but he will never be as strong as a good draft horse.

The important point to be understood is the simple fact that both types of horses will be both stronger and faster if you increase their muscular mass. And the same thing applies to bodybuilders and weightlifters.

Bodybuilders should get their muscles as strong as possible and weightlifters should get their muscles as large as possible. Stronger muscles are larger and larger muscles are stronger.

Some people believe that Frank Zane has ideal proportions for bodybuilding.

CHAPTER 4
NEGATIVE TRAINING— THE BEST KIND OF EXERCISE

Exercise is capable of producing a wide variety of results, such as increases in strength, improvement in flexibility, greater cardiovascular endurance, and a number of other physical improvements. All of these factors are important for even a normal degree of health, and particularly important for athletes.

In this chapter, however, attention will be directed toward only two of the possible results of exercise: the development of maximum strength and the simultaneous production of maximum flexibility. These two factors are unavoidably linked by the simple fact that the best program of exercises designed to produce strength will also promote flexibility. Research shows that stretching movements are an absolute requirement for building maximum strength, and that increased flexibility is a very valuable by-product of a properly designed strength program.

It should be noted that it is possible to increase flexibility while doing little in the way of building strength. And it should also be understood that many types of exercises will produce at least some degree of increased strength while doing nothing in the way of improving flexibility.

For the purpose of producing maximum strength, a muscle must be worked against resistance throughout its full range of possible movement. Resistance must be available in the position of full contraction—and resistance is also required in the position of full stretch. Unfortunately, most types of exercise provide no resistance at either end of the movement. As a result, a trainee's strength is increased only during the midrange of movement and his flexibility is not improved at all.

Examining Isokinetics

One highly advertised method of training which does nothing in the way of improving flexibility is called *isokinetics*. Isokinetics, according to its legal definition, is a type of dynamic exercise in

Negative-only chins and dips can be performed on the Nautilus multi-exercise machine by doing the positive work with your legs and the negative work with your arms.

The top position of a negative-only dip.

which movement velocity is held constant. Some manufacturers of isokinetic machines prefer to say that their devices provide *accommodating resistance,* since the resistance provided is supposed to be equal to and opposite to the applied force.

Regardless of what the isokinetic machines are called, exercises performed on them are based upon a speed-limiting device. No barbell plates or weights are used. Resistance is provided by some form of friction: mechanical, air, or liquid. The resistance is unavoidably linked to movement. When movement stops, the resistance ceases.

A moment's consideration makes it obvious that full-range exercise is impossible with isokinetics. Upon reaching a position of full contraction at the end of the exercise, additional movement is impossible. Since the availability of such resistance is linked to movement, a lack of movement means a total lack of resistance. Without resistance there is no exercise.

And at the start of the exercise there is no available resistance to provide the prestretching which is valuable for strength building. Prestretching of an extended muscle at the start of an exercise movement is provided by negative resistance, and the speed-limiting types of exercise devices have no negative resistance.

The Importance of Negative Resistance

Barbells and most other types of exercise devices are based upon negative resistance. When lifting a barbell you are performing positive work against negative resistance. You are pulling up and the barbell is providing resistance against your movement by pushing down.

A barbell also provides negative work. At the top of a movement, after the weight has been raised as high as possible, the barbell must be lowered back to the starting position. Thus, you

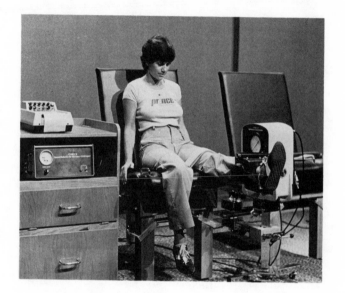

Shown about is an isokinetic machine which is set up to test or train the left quadriceps and hamstrings. To involve the right thigh, the trainee must reposition the unit and sit on the other side. *(Photo by Ellington Darden)*

are performing negative work while lowering the barbell.

A similar happening occurs with Nautilus equipment. Lifting the weight stack is positive work. Lowering the weight stack provides negative work to the involved muscles.

For the purpose of building strength, such lowering of weight is far more important than lifting weight.

If you remove negative resistance from an exercise, as the isokinetic people have done, you remove a large part of the strength-building characteristics of the exercise at the same time. And you destroy the flexibility-promoting factors. Such exercise, in spite of the claims by its promoters, will do little in the way of building strength, and nothing in the way of improving flexibility.

Muscular Soreness

The makers of such devices also point out that isokinetic exercises do not cause muscular soreness. And in this instance, at least, their claim is correct. The reason that isokinetic exercises do not produce muscular soreness is that they do not produce stretching.

When a muscle is first exposed to an actual full-range movement against resistance, the attachments will be forced into a position beyond the range of average movement. If part of the muscular structure is disproportionately weak, then the weak area will become sore as a result.

That weaker area will also become stronger as a result, and it will never become stronger until and unless it is exposed to such resistance.

With regular training, severe muscular soreness does not continue. Severe soreness occurs only at first, as a result of the first one or two training periods. Then it quickly disappears, and it will not return as long as regular training continues.

Positive or concentric work, as provided by

Lee Haney uses negative work to his advantage in all his workouts.

Exercises performed with a barbell provide both positive and negative work to the involved muscles.

isokinetic devices, involves only part of a muscular structure. It does nothing for the most important areas of movement, the fully contracted position and the fully stretched position.

Negative or eccentric work, as provided by a barbell or a Nautilus machine, exercises a far larger part of the total muscular structure—and does improve flexibility. Such exercises will produce muscular soreness at first, since this soreness is the unavoidable price of worthwhile results.

But an extreme degree of muscular soreness is not a requirement. If a break-in program of fairly light movements is followed for a period of a week at the start of training, then an uncomfortable degree of soreness will be avoided. After such a break-in program, severe muscular soreness will vanish and will not return regardless of the intensity of training.

Even a well-trained individual, however, may experience some degree of muscular soreness if he changes his exercises. Adding a new exercise to his program may involve stretching in an area of movement that is new even to an experienced trainee.

So even a well-conditioned trainee should break in gradually when adding a new exercise to his program.

If a trainee has been using a particular exercise for two or three weeks, or longer, then it is almost impossible to make him sore as a result of that exercise. He will not become sore from his regular workouts, regardless of the intensity of the workouts.

Isokinetic devices provide positive-only resistance. Barbells and Nautilus machines provide both positive and negative resistance. With an isokinetic device you are performing concentric contractions. With a barbell or Nautilus machine you perform both concentric and eccentric contractions.

Negative Work and Intensity

Careful research clearly proves that eccentric contractions, or negative exercises, are of far greater value for the purpose of building strength. When large groups of previously untrained individuals were trained with negative-only exercises the results were far better than those produced by a similar group trained with positive-only exercises.

The cause-and-effect factors involved in exercise are actually quite simple: Strength increases are produced in proportion to the intensity of an exercise.

Intensity is best defined as "percentage of momentary ability."

If you are capable of bench-pressing 300 pounds, and you press only 100 pounds, then the intensity is low. If you are capable of 300 pounds and you use 300 pounds, the intensity is high.

No amount of low-intensity training will produce much in the way of increases in strength. If the intensity is high, then a very small amount of training will quickly produce maximum strength.

High Intensity, But Low Force

The isokinetics people also claim that such training provides the highest possible intensity, a claim which is simply not true. But it is true that isokinetic exercises produce maximum force, which is neither necessary nor desirable.

Intensity produces results, force causes injuries.

A muscle is stimulated to grow only when it is exposed to an amount of resistance that is very close to its maximum level of momentary ability.

Injuries are caused when an amount of force is produced which exceeds the momentary breaking strength of some part of the muscular structure.

So the intensity of exercise must be as high as possible, but the force must be as low as possible.

It is easily possible to provide both maximum intensity and very little force at the same time.

EMG measurements of the electrical activity that occurs during muscular work clearly prove that the intensity of exercise is much higher during an eccentric contraction, while performing negative work, when lowering a weight. It is also obvious that the force is lower during negative work. Thus negative exercises provide both higher intensity and lower force.

Negative exercises do more in the way of stimulating strength increases—and do so while involving very little force. So negative exercises are both more productive and far safer.

If a 100-pound barbell is resting on a scale, the scale will indicate the full weight—proving that the barbell is producing 100 pounds of downward force.

If you grip the barbell and produce 50 pounds of upward force, the scale will then indicate only 50 pounds—proving that you are producing 50 pounds of force. But the barbell will not move.

If you then produce 100 pounds of upward force, the scale will read zero. Yet the barbell still won't move.

In order to move the barbell upward, you must produce force in excess of 100 pounds. If such movement is occurring, then this is clear proof that you are producing more than 100 pounds of force.

But if, instead of lifting the barbell, somebody handed you the weight in the top position, and if you simply lowered it instead of raising it, then it is also obvious that you would not be producing 100 pounds of force.

If you made no attempt to stop the downward movement, and no attempt to reverse the movement, then you would be producing less than 100 pounds of force. However, if you did stop the movement, then you would be producing exactly 100 pounds of force. If you reversed the movement, then you would be producing more than 100 pounds of force.

Obviously, then, the movement should never be stopped and should never be reversed. A continuous but slow downward movement should be permitted. Your muscles will thus be delaying the movement but will never stop it.

An understanding of the above simple points should make it obvious that this style of exercise will produce little force, and will thus be far safer than any other style of exercise. But what about the all-important factor of intensity?

If the weight is properly selected, then the intensity will be far higher in such exercises.

Performing Negative Repetitions

During the first two or three negative repetitions, it should be possible for the trainee to reverse the movement and move the weight in a positive direction. No attempt to do so should be made.

Then, during the next two or three repetitions, it should be possible to stop the movement. No attempt to do so should be made.

Only after several repetitions have been performed with no attempt to stop or reverse the movement—only after it becomes momentarily impossible to stop or reverse the movement—should the trainee even attempt to stop the movement.

In effect, if you can reverse the movement, don't try—and if you can even stop the movement, don't try.

After it becomes impossible to reverse or stop the movement, then try as hard as you can.

Undeniable Physical Laws

A negative style of training will result in an intensity that is impossible to duplicate while training with positive movements—and will do so while involving very little in the way of force.

The above points are not a matter of opinion.

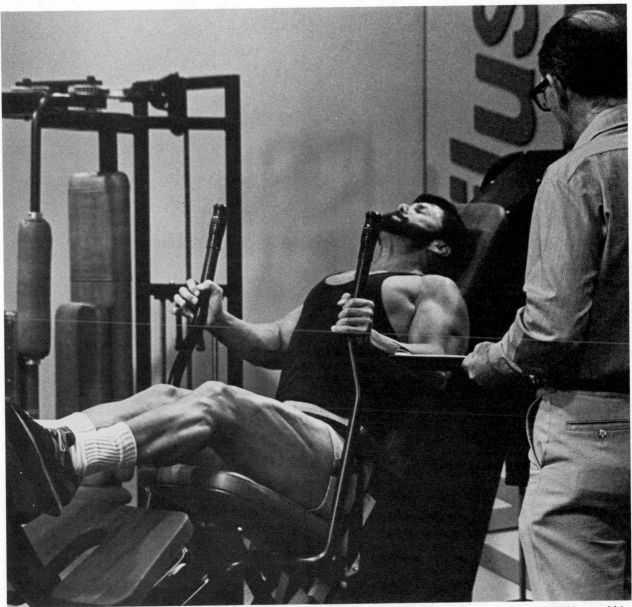

Boyer Coe performs the Nautilus decline press machine in a negative-only fashion. He uses his legs to do the lifting and his arms to do the lowering. *(Photo by Ellington Darden)*

They are not unproved theory. Instead, they are simple, undeniable, physical laws. The reader is, of course, perfectly free to form any opinion that he chooses. But remember, you cannot change the laws of physics to suit yourself.

That is exactly what the makers of isokinetic machines are trying to do. Having removed the most important part of exercise—the negative resistance—they are now pointing with claimed pride to the fact that their devices provide positive-only exercise, involve concentric-only contractions.

Failing to understand the actual factors involved, many people will be misled into believing the claims about isokinetic exercises. This is unfortunate, because the result will be that many people will thus be led in exactly the wrong direction.

The truth of the matter is that isokinetic movements are the worst type of exercises. They are the least productive type of exercise, and the most dangerous type of exercise.

If no other type of exercise were available, then, and only then, isokinetic exercises might be worth considering. It happens, however, that we do have a choice in the matter. It is ridiculous to use the worst type of exercise when it is possible to use the best type of exercise.

Negative-Only Research

Tom Laputka is a former professional football player who now works for Nautilus Sports/Medical Industries. In 1972, Tom was in one of the Nautilus research projects involving negative-only work.

"At that time in my life," Tom recalls, "I wanted to get as big and strong as possible. And I wanted the results as fast as possible. I had about three months to get in shape before the start of football camp.

"Arthur Jones challenged me to train with him in a negative-only fashion. I accepted the challenge and met him several days a week at a 30-year-old metal building behind the DeLand High School.

"Inside the building, there were wall-to-wall Nautilus machines, many of which were crude-looking compared to the machines sold today. The atmosphere in the place—well, it's unforgettable. It was dimly lit—you had trouble seeing across the room—and always reeked with damp, hot, smelly air. But, you know, the place was alive with excitement—muscle-building excitement.

"On training days, the entire room was filled with bodybuilders and weightlifters. And in the middle of it all was Arthur Jones doing the orchestration.

"For the negative-only training, we worked in groups of four. I needed two people, two strong people, to pull the movement arm to the contracted position—and another person, sometimes two, to stand on the weight stack while I slowly lowered the movement arm. I always tried to use a resistance that barely allowed 10 repetitions.

"My results? They were fantastic—the best I've ever experienced. My muscular size, strength, and endurance increased significantly as a result of almost every workout. When I reported to football camp, I weighed 263 pounds and had more muscle on my body than ever before. Furthermore, I was faster on my feet. That year, I played the best football of my career."

A listing of some of the incredible training poundage that Tom used in his negative-only workouts is as follows:

Hip and back (single movement-arm version)—700 pounds with one leg. That required the entire 500-pound weight stack plus a 200-pound man riding the stack. And he worked each hip separately.

Leg extension—500 pounds, which included a 300-pound weight stack and a 200-pound rider.

Leg curl—350 pounds, 150-pound weight stack and a 200-pound rider.

Pullover (plateloading version)—700 pounds, 300 pounds of plates and two 200-pound riders.

Dip—463 pounds, 263 pounds of bodyweight and 200 pounds around the hips.

Torso arm—350 pounds, 150-pound weight stack and a 200-pound rider.

Triceps extension (plateloading version)—150 pounds of plates.

Biceps curl (plateloading version)—150 pounds of plates.

"One important rule I learned from the research project," Tom says, "was that it was very easy to overtrain using negative-only exercise. For example, my strength plateaued after four weeks of training. That indicated to me that my strength had improved to the point that I was now overtraining. To make continued progress I had to reduce my workouts from three days a week to two days a week.

"A month later, my strength plateaued again. At the second plateau, I reduced my training from twice a week to three times every two weeks. Almost immediately my strength increased. I never reached a third plateau, as I had to report to football camp before the end of that month. Even then, my strength on some exercises was so great it was scary: 700 pounds on the hip and back, and that was with one leg only, and 700 pounds on the pullover.

"I've often wondered what would have happened after the next plateau. Or if I'd gone to once-a-week training. Arthur would have had to redesign some of the machines so we could get more helpers around them. Or we would have had to rent a forklift to do a majority of the lifting."

Many women are not strong enough to perform the positive portion of a dip. But they are strong enough to lower themselves slowly from the top position. Negative-only dips are one of the best exercises for a woman's upper body. *(Photo by Ellington Darden)*

Negative-Only Guidelines

For weeks at a time, we have had many of our trainees on a program strictly limited to negative-only resistance. The results have always been very significant.

In the meantime, we have been telling everybody we talk to about the enormous advantages of negative-only resistance. As a result of this spreading knowledge, thousands of people are now training in this fashion. From every report that we have received so far, all of these people are producing significant gains.

Many of our negative-only workouts are so brief that they are almost ridiculous. Many involve only one set of each of eight exercises—workouts that can be and should be finished in about 16 minutes.

Some people, probably quite a few people, will make the same old mistake of assuming that more is better. Please don't make that mistake. Brief workouts are a requirement. If you make the mistake of training more, then you will gain less. If you train too much, then you won't gain at all.

Negative-Only Problems

There are a few problems, however, with negative-only training.

First is the problem of strength, your own strength. You will become very strong, and quickly, from negative-only work. As a result, you will need to pin 25, 50, or even as much as 100 pounds onto the weight stacks of most Nautilus machines. This can become a nuisance.

Second is the problem of helpers. To perform negative-only work efficiently, you need the assistance of two strong men. These men must quickly push or pull the movement arms of the various Nautilus machines into the contracted position, so you can perform only the negative portion of the exercise. Such lifting soon becomes boring for even the most motivated of men.

Third is the problem of accurately recording

the intensity of your negative-only workouts. It is easy to get into the habit of resting too long between negative-only repetitions. Resting for only two or three seconds between repetitions gives your muscles time to temporarily recover. Rather than becoming stronger, you are simply learning how to cheat by lowering the level of intensity. Furthermore, it can become dangerous if you rest too long between repetitions. A 3-second rest between repetitions means that you are performing a series of single-attempt lifts. Such lifting can lead to poor form and a possible injury.

Problems one, two, and three can be solved by using negative-only training sparingly, perhaps once every two weeks. On your normal workouts, you can and you should emphasize the negative phase of each repetition by taking twice as long to lower the weight as it takes you to raise it. The tried-and-proved guideline to use on most Nautilus machines is as follows: *Lift the weight in 2 seconds, lower the weight in 4 seconds.*

The Negative Challenge

The simple logic, the physical laws, the theory, the research results, and the practical experience all indicate exactly the same thing: The best type of exercise is negative only. For maximum results, however, use it infrequently.

Arthur Jones observes Boyer Coe's form in the normal chinup. On any normal exercise, it is advantageous to perform the positive work in 2 seconds and the negative work in 4 seconds. *(Photo by Ellington Darden)*

CHAPTER 5
THE REVOLUTIONARY SQUAT MACHINE, PART A

From 1968 through 1975, Arthur Jones published a large number of exercise-related books and articles.

His *Nautilus Bulletin No. 1* and *No. 2* became instant best-sellers. His monthly training articles in *Iron Man* were eagerly read and applied by thousands of bodybuilders. His high-intensity-exercise philosophy—which was peppered with concepts such as negative-only, negative-accentuated, duo-poly, pre-exhaustion, and infimetrics—had added a much-needed shot of energy to the world of muscle building.

For the next six years, however, from 1975 through 1981, Jones published nothing.

Some people close to him said he had become bored with anything related to exercise. Other people said he had transferred his creativity to video productions. Yet others said he didn't have anything new or different to add to what he had already covered in detail.

But whatever the reasons behind Jones's leave of absence, he returned in 1982 with renewed enthusiasm. He definitely had something to say, and he said it as only Arthur Jones can.

This chapter and the next three were adapted from his comeback article, which was titled "From Here to Infinity, or Very Close: Featuring the Duo Squat Machine and Lower Back Machine."

Single- and Multiple-Joint Movements

A single-joint movement involves rotation around only one joint, or one axis of the body. The leg extension, leg curl, calf raise, and wrist curl are examples of single-joint movements.

A multiple-joint exercise provides movement around two or more joints or axes. Examples of multiple-joint exercises are the bench press, overhead press, leg press, and squat.

Everything else being equal, a multiple-joint movement is a more productive exercise than a single-joint movement. The simple reason is that it

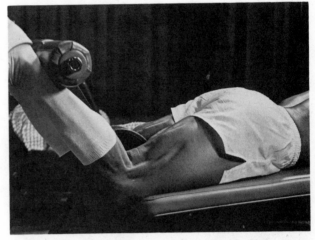

The leg curl is a single-joint movement that involves rotation around the knee. *(Photo by Inge Cook)*

The leg press is a multiple-joint movement that involves rotation around the hip, knee, and ankle.

Boyer Coe and Ellington Darden examine an oversize drawing of the Nautilus duo squat machine.

involves more muscle mass. A barbell squat, therefore, is a more productive overall exercise than a barbell curl.

Carefully note the qualification: *everything else being equal.* The problem is that everything else isn't equal.

Examining the Curl

With the use of a cam, the first Nautilus biceps curling machine produced an enormous increase in the productivity of this exercise when it was compared to a curl performed with a barbell.

Why? And how?

Because by providing a source of resistance throughout the entire range of movement, the Nautilus curling machine produced resistance for the total length of the muscles involved in bending your arms.

And secondly, because the cam varied the resistance properly throughout the entire range of movement.

As a result, the Nautilus curling machine was the first machine of its kind to provide full-range resistance for the biceps of the upper arm.

In contrast, a barbell curl does not provide resistance throughout the entire movement. The resistance that is provided in a barbell curl does not vary properly, does not vary in proportion to the actual need for variable resistance.

A barbell curl works the bending muscles of your arms only in the midrange of possible movement. As a result, it produces a peaked strength curve: strong in the middle, but weak on both ends.

So a barbell curl provides variable resistance, but the variation in resistance that is provided by a barbell has nothing to do with the variation in resistance that is actually required for the proper development of your muscles.

The variation in resistance that is provided by a barbell is random. The variation in resistance that

Sergio Oliva is using an early model of the Nautilus combination biceps/triceps machine. This was the first machine to provide full-range resistance for the biceps and triceps. *(Photo by Inge Cook)*

Shown above is the squat machine that was used during the 1973 Colorado Experiment. This machine was used in a double-legged manner. *(Photo by Inge Cook)*

is required for the proper development of your muscles is specific.

In one or two unimportant exercises, the random resistance that is provided by a barbell is so close to being right that it would be difficult to improve the exercise to any significant degree. The best example of this random variation is the wrist curl.

But that is an exception, not the rule.

Examining the Squat

In 1973, Arthur Jones built a squat machine for use during the Colorado Experiment. A few months later, he built a second version of this machine. The second machine was used in 1975, during an experiment at the Military Academy in West Point.

Neither of these machines was ever manufactured for sale to the general public. Both versions still left a great deal to be desired. We simply did not know how to vary the resistance properly in the squat. And Jones still believed that it was impossible to vary the resistance properly during a multiple-joint exercise.

In 1982, however, thanks to the negative cam, Nautilus began manufacturing a squat machine.

Improving an exercise such as the curl is one thing. Producing an equal degree of improvement in an exercise such as the squat is an entirely different matter, for a number of reasons.

In a curl, or in any single-joint exercise, you are dealing with degrees of rotation. You are concerned with rotational movement around one axis of the body.

In a squat, or in any multiple-joint exercise, you are dealing with a relatively straight line of movement. A straight line of movement is a resultant of the rotational movements around two or more points.

Your strength varies during both types of movements, so variation in the resistance is required

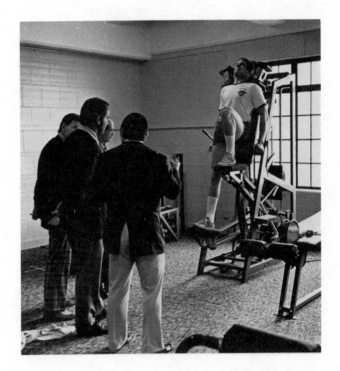

In 1975, Arthur Jones built an improved version of the squat machine for the training of cadets at the United States Military Academy at West Point, New York. The exercise was performed standing, but, unlike the earlier model, this machine was used by alternating legs. *(Photo by Inge Cook)*

during both multiple-axis and single-axis exercises. But here the similarities cease and the problems start.

First, your strength varies much more in a multiple-joint movement than it does in a single-joint movement.

Second, the pattern of variation is much different.

In a curl, the required resistance increases during the first part of the movement and then decreases during the last part of the movement. It goes up, reaches a peak, and then goes back down.

In a squat, the proper resistance must start fairly high, go down as you approach the so-called sticking point, and then increase rapidly when the sticking point is passed.

Third, during a properly performed curl, the muscles remain under load throughout the movement. The resistance is not removed from the muscles at the top of the movement.

Whereas in a squat, the resistance is removed from the muscles in the top position. A point of lockout is reached where the load is supported entirely by your bones.

A careful examination of the following graph will make several of these differences obvious. The dotted line represents your strength curve during a curl. The heavy, solid line represents your strength curve during a squat.

Cam Action

A normal cam, a positive cam, can easily provide the variation in resistance that is required in the curl. A positive cam, however, cannot begin to provide the variation in resistance that is required in the squat.

But a negative cam can.

The resistance varies less than 50 percent in a properly designed curling machine, and a positive cam is easily capable of providing that de-

STRENGTH CURVES: SQUAT VS. CURL

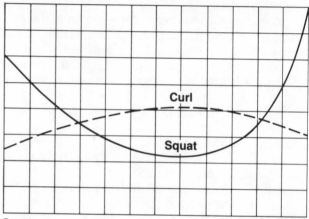

Starting Position   **Finishing Position**

The graph above shows the differences in the patterns of the strength curves involved in the squat and curl. Please note that these are not actual strength curves. The actual strength curves would vary much more than is shown.

The sticking point in the barbell squat is when the thighs are parallel to the floor.

gree of variation. Yet your strength varies by several hundred percent during a squat, and a positive cam cannot meet the requirements.

While it is certainly true that a cam is the only practical way to provide properly the variation in resistance that is required in exercise, it does not follow that the addition of a cam will automatically improve an exercise machine.

The cam must be right, must provide the proper variation in resistance required by a particular movement. The variation in resistance that is right in one movement is utterly wrong in any other movement. Each movement has a very distinct strength curve.

So each movement requires a different cam. But a cam can be different while still being wrong.

And how do you know that a cam is right? By the results!

Eliminating the Sticking Point

During the performance of almost all barbell exercises, you will encounter a point in the movement where the resistance feels very heavy. This position is called the sticking point.

You will also encounter one or more positions during the movement where the resistance feels very light, or where the resistance falls off literally to nothing.

And it does not matter how long you train with a barbell, you will always encounter the same sticking points, and the same points of little or no resistance.

So it is obvious that the random variation in resistance that is provided by a barbell does not match the need for variation that is actually required.

Well, you might say, then all you need to do is to test the actual strength curves of one or more people and then build a machine that provides the same variation in resistance.

That won't work either, because the actual strength curve has little to do with the potential strength curve. What it does not indicate is what it can be, or should be.

Giving a reading test to an unschooled subject might tell you what his reading ability was at the moment, but it would tell you nothing about his potential.

And giving the same test to a subject who had been taught improperly might give you even worse results.

It's the same when it comes to strength tests. Any sort of test you can think of is worthless for the purpose of determining what the strength curve of a person can be, and should be.

In any case, apart from the highly sophisticated, one-of-a-kind equipment that was developed by Nautilus, nobody else in the world has the ability to accurately measure strength curves. One such tool, an isokinetic device, that has been on the market for several years was recently shown to be in error by as much as 520 percent.

Arthur Jones first became aware of the need for variation in the resistance in exercise in 1939. It then took him 30 years to figure out what the actual variation in resistance should be. "In the end," says Jones, "the solution was so simple that it should have been obvious to me from the start . . . one of those why-didn't-I-think-of-that-sooner type of things."

Your strength will never accommodate itself to the improper variation in resistance that is provided by a barbell, and the same thing is true in regard to an exercise machine that provides the wrong variation in resistance. But your strength will accommodate itself to the variation in resistance that is provided by an exercise machine that provides the proper variation in resistance.

When you first use a Nautilus machine, it is almost certain that you will encounter an area in the movement where the resistance will feel too heavy. It is also possible that you may encounter one or more positions where the resistance may feel too light.

That situation, however, will change and very quickly, whereas with a barbell or with another type of exercise machine it will never change.

Within a very short space of time, the resistance provided by a Nautilus machine will feel perfectly smooth. The resistance will feel the same in every position throughout a full range of movement. It will feel the same in every position in spite of the fact that the resistance is constantly changing. The changes in resistance will be in exact proportion to your changes in strength.

If the variation in resistance is wrong, then it will never feel smooth. But when it is right, it will feel smooth.

Proper Strength Curves

During an experiment at the United States Military Academy in 1975, we found that the dynamic strength of a group of cadets increased by 60 percent in one movement within a period of less than six weeks. They could perform a full-range movement with 60 percent more weight.

However, their static strength increased only 6 percent at their strongest point in the movement.

Some people, therefore, might believe that there is no relationship between dynamic strength and static strength. If so, they are wrong.

Because we also found that the same subjects increased their static strength in the starting position of the movement by exactly 100 percent, and their static strength in the finishing position of the movement by 140 percent.

The graph below will make these points clear: The dotted line represents the starting strength curve, and the heavy, solid line represents the finishing strength curve.

You will also notice that the final strength curve was much flatter than the starting strength curve.

While it is true that a perfect strength curve in

THE RESULTS OF SIX WEEKS OF NAUTILUS EXERCISE ON THE STRENGTH CURVE OF ONE MAJOR MUSCLE.

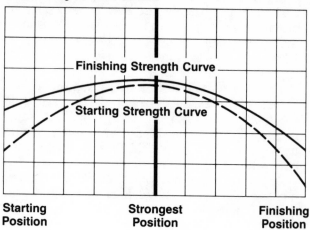

Finishing Strength Curve

Starting Strength Curve

Starting Position   Strongest Position   Finishing Position

this movement will never be totally flat, it is also true that the starting strength curve of these cadets was peaked much too high in the midrange of the movement. The curve was too high in proportion to their strength in the starting position, or in the finishing position. This was the result of training with exercises that provided little in the way of meaningful resistance at either the start or the finish of the movement.

So six weeks of proper training increased their strength in their strongest position by only 6 percent, an average of approximately 1 percent per week. But in their weakest position, proper training increased their strength by 140 percent, an average of approximately 23 percent per week.

Why?

Because as a result of their previous training, they were already quite strong in the midrange of movement, while being very weak near both ends of the movement. Thus when they were first exposed to a form of resistance that provided a proper variation in resistance throughout a full range of possible movement, they were limited to an amount of weight that they could handle in their weakest position.

The result was that their strength in their weaker positions increased at a very rapid rate, while the strength in their strongest position changed very little.

When a proper strength curve has been established, then additional increases in strength will be produced in proportion throughout a full range of movement. This is another proof that the variation in resistance that is provided is proper for the movement.

At that point, the resistance will feel perfectly smooth. It will feel the same in every position throughout a full range of possible movement.

By the end of the program, these cadets were very close to a perfect strength curve in this exercise. If the program had been continued longer, and if they had produced, for example, an additional increase in strength of 20 percent in any one position, then they would have produced an increase of approximately 20 percent in every position.

From that point on, any increases in static strength would have been matched exactly by increases in dynamic strength.

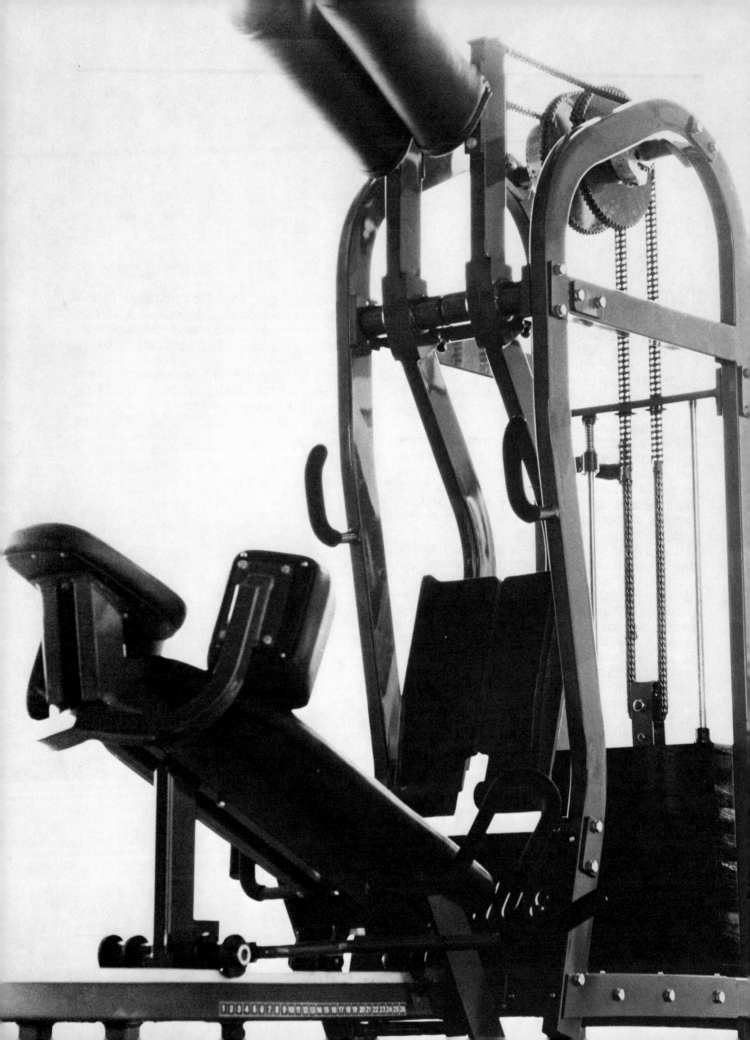

CHAPTER 6
THE REVOLUTIONARY SQUAT MACHINE, PART B

A Nautilus machine is an improved barbell, a logical barbell, a rational barbell. With a barbell you are lifting weights, and with a Nautilus machine you are lifting weights. The major differences are that a Nautilus machine provides your muscles with the required overload throughout the movement, and that the variation in resistance provided by a Nautilus machine is based upon the actual requirements of the muscles themselves, rather than being arbitrarily dictated by the random variation in resistance provided by a barbell.

Since 1970, Nautilus has been marketing a wide variety of machines that provide greater range of movement and variable resistance in a manner that is so close to being perfect that any slightest imperfection is of no practical importance. The increased range of movement results from the overall structure of the machines and from the greatly improved variation in resistance provided by the cams.

During those years, Arthur Jones and Nautilus made a number of other very important contributions to the field of exercise. Nautilus was the first to point out the real value of the negative part of an exercise, while a number of other people were doing everything possible to convince the public that the negative part of exercise was of no value, was dangerous.

Nautilus also introduced negative-accentuated exercise, lifting the resistance with two limbs and lowering it with one; hyper exercise, working both positive and negative strengths to failure; infimetric exercise, moving the restraining bar in place and removing the selector pin to allow the negative-contracting limb infinite resistance for the positive-contracting limb; and akinetic exercise, the same as infimetric except that a predetermined amount of resistance is used on the weight stack.

The progress of Nautilus has been continuous over the last 13 years, continuous and evolutionary. But perhaps not revolutionary. Not truly revolutionary since the initial introduction of the first Nautilus machines placed on the market; not, at least, until very recently, until Arthur Jones finally understood the actual potential of the negative cam.

The proper application of the negative cam is nothing short of revolutionary. The negative cam makes it possible to design an exercise machine for a multiple-joint movement that provides all but one of the features already incorporated into Nautilus machines designed for single-joint movements.

There are at least nine requirements for a proper full-range exercise. These requirements are as follows:

1. A rotational form of resistance, rotating on a common axis with the involved joint of the body

2. A direct form of resistance—resistance that is directly imposed upon the body part that is being moved by the muscles being worked

3. An automatically variable form of resistance that varies instantly as movement occurs

4. Balanced resistance that varies in accordance with the actual requirements of the muscles in different positions

5. Resistance that is provided in a stretched starting position, which requires a range of movement in the machine that actually exceeds the possible range of movement of the user

6. Negative work potential

7. Positive work potential

8. Prestretching, a factor that is required during the last one or two repetitions of a set of high-intensity movements

9. Resistance that is provided in the finishing position of the movement, the only position of full-muscular contract

A tenth factor may or may not be a requirement for truly proper, full-range, high-intensity ex-

The Nautilus duo squat machine is a vast improvement over the barbell squat.

ercise—this being an unrestricted speed of movement.

All of the ten factors have been provided in almost all Nautilus machines designed for single-joint movements. But please note the above qualification, "in almost all." The sentence does not read "in all Nautilus machines designed for single-joint movements." One of the ten factors is potentially dangerous in at least one movement. And for that reason, that feature is excluded from one of the single-axis Nautilus machines: the leg extension. The feature that is missing is number 5 in the above list, resistance that is provided in a stretched starting position.

Analyzing the Leg Extension

In the leg extension exercise, a truly full-range movement cannot be provided in a safe manner; attempting to do so may cause damage to the knee.

In that movement, when the muscle mass on the back of the calf comes into solid contact with the rear of the thigh while under a heavy load, then the effective axis of rotation can move a distance of as much as several inches. The knee is no longer rotating in a normal manner, and as a result, the ligaments and tendons of the knee are being stretched in a dangerous fashion.

So, for those very good reasons, the Nautilus leg extension machine does not provide one of the features actually required for full-range exercise. Stretching is fine in most movements, to a reasonable degree at least and when it is done in a safe manner, but stretching the ligaments of the knee is neither safe nor desirable.

Analyzing the Squat

It has been pointed out for years that squatting to a low position could cause damage to the knees, damage very similar in nature to the damage that can possibly result from doing leg extensions with

The Nautilus leg extension does not cause excessive stretching of the knees in the starting position. *(Photo by Ellington Darden)*

The squat has long been recognized as the single most productive barbell exercise. *(Photo by Inge Cook)*

an extreme range of movement.

While it is possible to hurt yourself as a result of doing squats incorrectly, the squat is undoubtedly the single most productive barbell exercise.

The squat is productive because it involves a far greater mass of muscle than any other exercise. It uses the largest and most powerful muscles in the body, the buttocks, plus the large muscles of the frontal thigh, plus the muscles of the lower legs, plus the muscles of the lower back, as well as a number of other muscles.

Because of the sheer mass of the muscles that are involved in the squat, and the need to use heavy resistance to overload these muscles properly, it follows that the squat has never had the reputation of being an easy exercise. In fact, properly performed, the squat is the hardest exercise that you will ever find. The hardest, and the most productive.

The problem then becomes one of attempting to realize the potential opportunity while simultaneously avoiding the potential danger. This is a problem that has been given a rather large share of Arthur Jones's attention for 12 years, and some of his attention for 30 years before that. Until recently he did not believe the problem could be solved in a really practical manner.

Recognizing the Problems

Three distinct but interrelated problems were involved. One, since the strength curve in a squat is so complex, it appeared to be impossible to vary the resistance properly. Two, since the movement of the feet during a squat is in an approximately straight line (although this "straight" movement is a resultant of rotational movements around three points), and since it was essential to produce this straight-line movement with a machine that was in fact rotational, the exact design of the movement arms of the machine was critical. Three, the torque of the movement arms had to be transmitted properly to the weight stack.

All of these things had to be done in a simple, reliable, and safe manner while keeping the friction to a minimum.

Furthermore, the machine had to be easy to get into and safe to get out of, no small problem in itself when you think about the range of movement involved in a full squat. Remember, with a barbell, you start a squat in the top position. But don't forget that first you had to get the weight up into that top position.

When you finish a barbell squat, you put the weight back onto a rack, again in the top position. Or at least you should, and you may well be in trouble if you can't. Did you ever get stuck in the low position of a barbell squat with 500 pounds on your back and no spotters? Lots of luck.

But equally important, how do you lift the 500 pounds into the top position in a machine before you start the exercise?

And when you have finished the exercise, what happens if you are exhausted and cannot get the weight back up into the top position? Then how do you get out of the machine, with both knees shoved back alongside your ears and a load of several hundred pounds wedging you into that position like a big sardine in a small can?

Arthur Jones not only preserved the productive capabilities of the squat but he enormously improved them while removing all of the dangers.

It is Jones's opinion that the new Nautilus duo squat machine provides the most productive exercise in history, by far. In fact, it is impossible to compare the exercise provided by this machine with any other known exercise.

And much of the thanks goes to the negative cam.

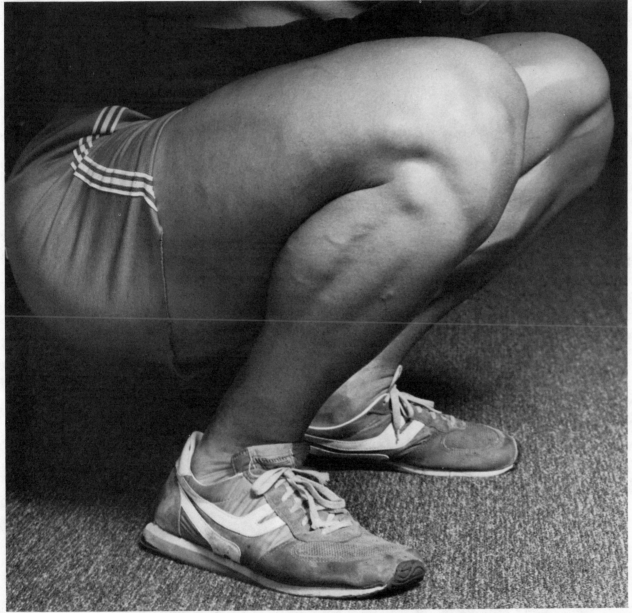

The low squat with a barbell, while productive, can overstretch the delicate ligaments of the knee.

CHAPTER 7
THE REVOLUTIONARY SQUAT MACHINE, PART C

A negative cam has the ability to properly vary the resistance during a multiple-joint exercise with none of the impossible problems associated with positive cams, or levers.

A normal cam, a positive cam, varies the resistance during exercise by changing its radius as it turns, thereby changing the lever, thus increasing or decreasing the torque. With a positive cam, the weight remains constant while the lever and the torque are changing as movement occurs. The torque goes up or down in exact proportion to changes in the lever.

The larger the radius of a positive cam, the greater the torque and the higher the resistance. The smaller the radius, the lower the resistance.

The above facts are all you need to design a perfect exercise for a single-joint movement such as a curl—provided you know the proper shape for the cam, as well as a few dozen other necessary bits and pieces of required information, since the cam cannot operate in a vacuum.

A positive cam can properly vary the resistance in any single-joint exercise. But a positive cam cannot begin to vary the resistance properly in a multiple-joint exercise such as the squat.

Why?

Because the resistance varies so much and so quickly that it is impossible to design a positive cam with the required shape.

When you start up from the low position of a full squat, your strength is fairly high, so you need a lot of resistance. As you move upward you become steadily weaker, so the resistance must be reduced in exact proportion to your decreasing strength. Then, when you reach the sticking point, your strength is at its lowest level, so the resistance must be low at this point. When you have passed the sticking point on your way up, your strength starts to increase very rapidly, and continues to increase rapidly throughout the rest of the movement. So the resistance must also increase in exact proportion, must increase several hundred percent in a very short distance.

The unavoidable result is that you are forced to lift an amount of weight that you can handle in your weakest position, which is nowhere near enough resistance in your strongest position.

A positive cam designed to provide that pattern and degree of variation would look a lot like an enormous banana, and the functional perimeter would have a concave shape. This is an obvious contradiction of terminology, because if the perimeter had the correct shape, then it wouldn't be functional, could not be functional.

Shortcomings of the Positive Cam

The basic problem with a positive cam in this application stems from the fact that a positive cam varies the torque by changing the lever. Thus the required resistance in a squat increases so rapidly that it is impossible to increase the radius of the cam to the required degree while maintaining a functional shape.

A negative cam, however, does not vary the torque. Instead, it maintains a constant level of torque while changing the force in inverse proportion to the radius of the cam.

If a positive cam that was capable of providing the required torque was mounted on the axis of the movement arms of our new squat machine, then the radius of that cam would have to be approximately 70 inches, nearly 6 feet. Remember, that is the radius, not the diameter, which would mean that the machine would be about 12 feet tall.

The radius of the negative cam used in the Nautilus duo squat machine is only a few inches. In fact, this is one of the smallest cams Nautilus has ever used.

With a positive cam, the resistance rises in proportion to increases in the size of the radius. With a

A close view of the negative cam as it unwinds. *(Photo by Lewis Green)*

negative cam, the resistance rises in inverse proportion to the size of the radius.

With a positive cam, larger is heavier. With a negative cam, smaller is heavier.

A positive cam winds. A negative cam unwinds.

The smaller the radius of a negative cam becomes, the higher the force rises. Apart from the limitations imposed by the structural strength of your materials, there is literally no limit to the force that you can produce with a negative cam.

You will reach the limits of your body long before you even begin to approach the limits of a negative cam. A negative cam can literally give you all the force you can tolerate, a billion times over, and still not even begin to approach its own limit. It has no limit.

Your Body's Structural Limits

While it is certainly true that your strength is very high near the top position of a squat, it is also true that your bones will not support an infinite weight. So Nautilus designed the negative cams in the new squat machine with this limitation clearly in mind. The maximum force, using the entire weight of 510 pounds, is approximately 1,174 pounds as you reach the finishing position of the squat. This is approximately equal to doing the last part of a barbell squat with 1,000 pounds, which amount of resistance is enough for anybody short of Paul Anderson.

As you move close to the finishing position of a squat, your muscles are given an enormous advantage of leverage. Even a man of average strength can perform the last part of a barbell squat with a weight of 1,000 pounds, if his bones can stand the load. But he had better not make the mistake of bending his legs very far under that kind of a load. If he does, he will not be able to stop the downward movement and will hit the floor so fast and so hard that he will no longer be even slightly interested in exercise, or anything else for that matter.

Solving the Primary Problems

You will not encounter that problem in our new squat machine, because the resistance will instantly and automatically change in proportion to your strength in every position. There is no sticking point in the squat machine, and there is no point in the movement where the resistance is too light.

At the end of the movement, your legs will eventually reach a locked-out position, with the resistance removed from your muscles and entirely supported by your bones. Thus it is not possible to provide one of the requirements for a truly full-range exercise: resistance at the point of full muscular contraction.

Furthermore, the squat is not a rotational movement, as is a curl. This problem, however, has been solved by converting the straight-line movement of your feet to a rotational movement of the machine in such a manner that all of the benefits of a rotational movement are achieved while any potential problems are avoided. So we have the best features of both types of movements and the problems of neither.

What are the problems in a rotational movement?

There are no problems in most single-joint rotational movements. But don't forget about the problem that can be caused by trying to do a full-range leg extension.

Because of the way the lower leg comes into contact with the back of the thigh when the leg is bent to its limit at the knee, and because of the direction from which the resistance is imposed in that exercise, it is dangerous to perform a full-range leg extension with a heavy load.

Stretching the ligaments of the knee is also a very real danger when performing full squats with a barbell. The Nautilus duo squat machine corrects this problem and eliminates the danger of the low position. There is very little force in the direction that would cause the ligaments of the knees to stretch.

In the very low position of the squat in this machine, the forces on the knees are acting in a different direction from the forces that are dangerous to your knees in a barbell squat.

In a full-range leg extension movement, the force is acting at a right angle to the bones in your lower leg. When the back of your calf touches solidly against the back of your thigh, the force is doing two things: trying to bend the bones of your lower leg and trying to pull your knee apart.

In a barbell squat, in the low position, the force is acting at a somewhat different angle. In this case it is no longer imposed at a right angle to the bones of your lower leg. But it is still doing the same two things: trying to bend the bones of your lower leg and trying to pull your knee apart.

The direction of the force is much worse in the leg extension exercise than it is in the barbell squat. The amount of the force is much greater, and thus worse, in the squat. So the result is much the same in either case.

The situation is entirely different in the new Nautilus duo squat machine. The force is imposed from a much different direction in the low position of the squat, regardless of how low you go.

In this machine, in the low position, the force is imposed in line with the bones of your lower legs. Thus the force is not trying to bend the bones of your lower legs, nor is is trying to pull your knees apart.

The danger in a full squat, a low squat, is not a result of the position of your legs in relation to your torso. The danger is a result of the direction from which the force is imposed.

With the Nautilus duo squat machine, you can scratch one more danger off the list of problems involved in barbell squats, while adding a range

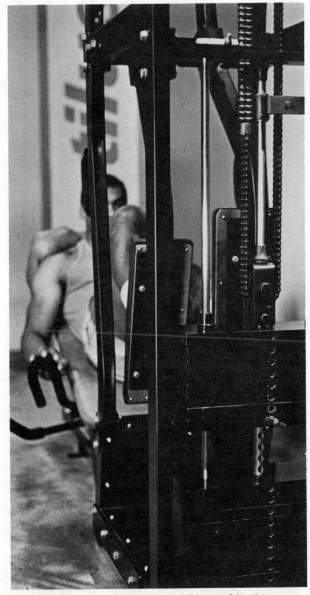

The duo squat machine can be used in an akinetic manner by placing the movement-restraining bar into the center position. *(Photo by Lewis Green)*

of movement that is impossible with a barbell.

Solving Additional Problems

The machine is entered in the midrange of possible movement, so if you are flexible enough to sit down in a chair then you can get into this machine with ease.

What about getting stuck under a heavy load in the bottom position? Impossible, because the duo squat is performed one leg at a time. In the event that you could not move the working leg out of the low position, you would simply bend the other leg and the weight would instantly be removed from both legs.

Bending your back under a heavy load? Perhaps not impossible if you really tried, but difficult. Your back is solidly supported against a strong, flat, comfortable surface in such a manner that bending the back is no longer a consideration.

Falling either forward or backward as a result of losing your balance? Impossible.

Oh, you don't like doing your squats one leg at a time? Why not? There are several advantages. Still, if you just must do them with both legs at the same time, then you can perform normal, parallel-position squats with both legs.

But, you say, in a parallel squat, 510 pounds of weight won't be enough. Don't bet on it until you have tried it. Remember, we have the negative cams working for us here. Just wait until you experience what a negative cam can do to 510 pounds. The force in the finishing position is approximately 1,174 pounds.

The duo squat machine can give you all the load you can handle, and then some—because we have added the feature of akinetic exercise to this machine, which simply means that you will be provided with literally any level of resistance that you can handle. Furthermore, you can perform the movements at any speed of movement without producing kinetic energy, which means that the

weight will never "float" upward as a result of kinetic energy created by a sudden movement, regardless of how fast you move.

Performing the Duo Squat Machine

The following directions and pictures apply to performing the duo squat machine in the normal, alternating manner.

Benefits of the Duo Squat Machine

One of the most important features of this machine is that it loads the muscles of the frontal thigh right up to the point of lockout. This means that the parts of the quadriceps that are the most important for the purpose of stabilizing the knee are being worked properly in a multiple-joint movement—for the first time in the history of exercise.

As it happens, this part of the muscle is very important for the purpose of preventing injuries, particularly in football.

But the benefits to be derived from this machine are not limited to the quadriceps. Equal benefits will be produced in the strongest muscles of the body, the gluteus maximus of the buttocks; in the thigh biceps or hamstrings muscles; in the lower back muscles; and in a number of smaller muscles.

As a means of gaining overall body strength and mass, this machine is by far the single best exercise device ever produced.

With all of the problems and with all of the dangers, the barbell squat has certainly been the most productive exercise in history. But it isn't anymore. The single most productive exercise is now provided by the duo squat machine from Nautilus.

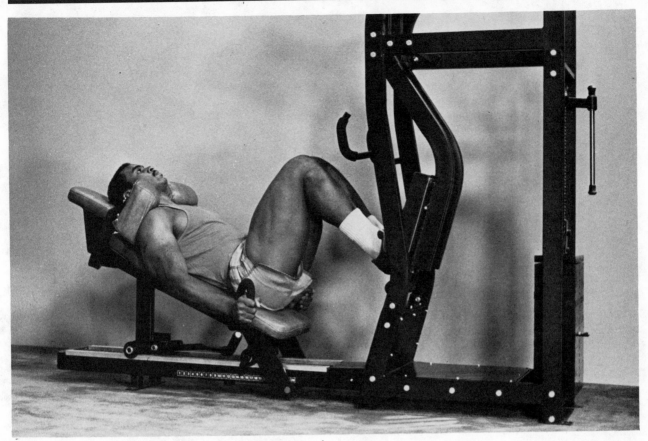

1. Sit on lower portion of seat. Shoulders should be under pads.
2. Place both feet at same time on movement arms. Heels should be on bottom of foot pedals.
3. Pull up on lower right handle to adjust seat carriage. Seat is in proper position when these three factors occur as both legs straighten: (a) negative cam fully unwinds, (b) movement arms touch crossbar, and (c) legs can barely lock out.

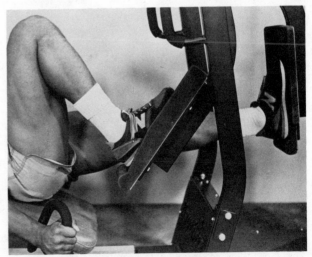

4. Straighten both legs. Keep head and shoulders on pads and hands on handles.

5. Hold left leg straight while right leg slowly bends and comes back as far as possible.
6. Push out smoothly with right until straight.
7. Hold right leg straight and bend left leg.
8. Push out smoothly with left leg until straight.
9. Alternate between right and left legs until fatigued.
(Photos by Lewis Green)

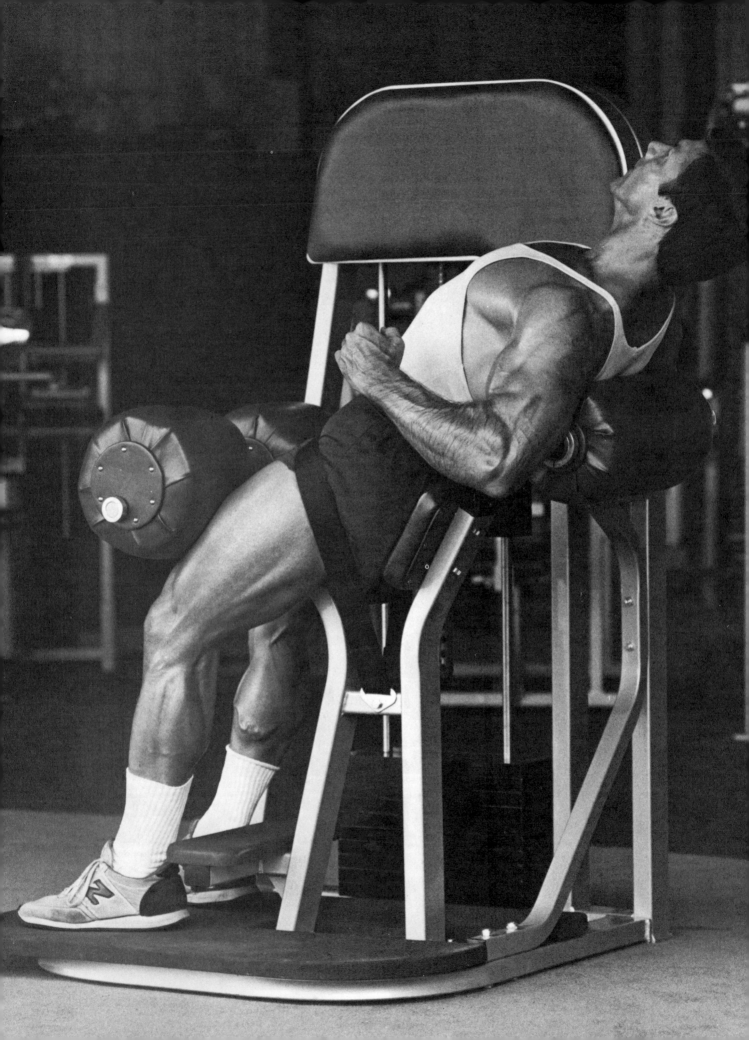

CHAPTER 8
THE LOWER BACK MACHINE

The lower back is one of the most important areas of the body, an area that is generally neglected. Furthermore, neglecting the lower back often leads to trouble.

If you happen to be one of those rare people who have never suffered from problems associated with the lower back, then the importance of this subject may be lost on you, for the moment. But the odds of enjoying a lifetime of such bliss are against you.

Sooner or later, if you live long enough, the odds are probably about ten to one that you will have trouble with your lower back. If you do, then you will appreciate the importance of this subject.

When your lower back is hurting, then nothing else works very well either—even if you feel like doing something that doesn't involve the lower back.

A very large part of these problems can be prevented, and they should be prevented, but they seldom are. Instead, most people ignore the lower back until it gives them trouble. A bumper sticker displayed an attitude that many people have: "Just ignore your teeth and they will go away."

Ignoring your lower back may not cause it to go away, but ignore it long enough and your ability to use it will certainly go away.

Beware of Advice
The muscles that provide the required strength in your lower back need exercise, just as does any other muscle in your body. Without that exercise they react like the rest of your muscles—they quietly go away, not entirely, perhaps, but to the point that they are no longer capable of doing their job.

When this happens, and it will if you neglect these muscles, then it is usually just a matter of time until you are in for a very rude surprise.

Yet you have been told repeatedly, since you

Casey Viator has not ignored his lower back development.

The contracted position of the Nautilus lower back machine.

were old enough to understand, not to lift with your back: "Use your legs, don't strain your back."

"Having heard that same advice for 50 years," writes Arthur Jones, "and having given the matter a great deal of thought for over 40 years, I still haven't been able to figure out how to do it. When I tried lifting something in the style suggested by this advice I always managed to hit my head on the concrete when I fell over backward."

Jones is not alone in his lifting experiences. Falling over backward results from the fact that you have only two legs, and the fact that you have to maintain your balance on those two legs while lifting. In reality, this means that you simply cannot lift anything of any consequence without bending your back.

Oh, you say, but you should bend at the hips, keep your back straight, and lift with your legs.

That is difficult to do unless the weight is very light. Even if you can lift in that fashion, the muscles of your back are still required to keep your back straight.

The consequence of such well-intentioned but misdirected advice is usually the opposite of the intended result. The muscles of the lower back need exercise, and the strength of your lower back is much more important than the size of your arms. If your lower back is causing you severe pain, you won't care how big your arms are.

Avoid Sudden Movements

Over the years, quite a variety of exercises have been tried: deadlifts, stiff-legged deadlifts, cleans, good-mornings, hyperextensions using your own bodyweight, and a number of other movements intended to strengthen the muscles of the lower back. None of these exercises really fills the bill, and all of the movements frequently lead to trouble.

Recently, thousands of bodybuilders, football players, and other athletes have been advised to practice such lifts as the power clean as an exercise to strengthen the lower back. This advice is nothing short of criminal malpractice regardless of the source. Power cleans have probably ruined at least a thousand backs for each one they have helped.

The next time somebody tells you to move quickly during exercise, to produce a sudden or jerky movement against resistance, then smile and walk away. The facts show that you are talking to a fool. Ignoring such advice may well be the most important thing you should remember about exercise, any exercise, but particularly an exercise involving the muscles of your lower back.

Sudden movements of the back are directly responsible for killing a few thousand people every year, and the backs that have been ruined by such movements number in the millions. Did you ever hear of whiplash?

Well, you can get whiplash just as quickly in the lower back as you can in the neck, and the result is frequently the same. You can get a whiplash of the lower back just as easily from a power clean as you can from a car wreck.

The problem of neck injuries in football could be solved by incorporating the helmet into the shoulder pads in such a fashion that the neck was totally protected. This would solve one problem and create an even bigger problem, because the forces would then be transmitted directly to the lower back. The nature of the game being what it is, there would be even more "spearing" than we have now, and many broken backs.

Controlling Force

Force is force, and your body doesn't know what the source of the force may be—the result is the same in any case. Once again, the facts show that sudden movement against resistance creates an enormous level of force.

An injury is caused when a force is imposed on

the body, a force that exceeds the momentary structural integrity of some part of the body. It's just that simple.

Yet, at the same time, your body requires force within reasonable levels. If the force of gravity is removed from your body for even a few days, the body reacts to this abnormal situation by starting to demineralize the bones. This reaction has created a serious problem for astronauts in the weightless environment of outer space, where exercise becomes a matter of life or death.

Your muscles also require force, and they react to a lack of force by a loss of both size and strength.

So the force must be at least high enough to maintain the normal level of minerals in your bones, and it must be at least high enough to maintain the strength of your muscles. But it must not be high enough to rip your muscles out by the roots or break your bones. Sudden or jerky movements against resistance can do both.

Even jogging involves G forces of as much as three times normal gravity, which means that a 200-pound man may experience a force of 600 pounds when his foot strikes the ground. Imagine what happens when you suddenly move a barbell, perhaps creating G forces that can reach a level fifteen times as high as normal gravity, G forces into the thousands of pounds?

All of these dangers can be avoided by the use of common sense, which often seems to be in short supply in some circles in the field of exercise.

High levels of force caused by a sudden movement are probably responsible for almost 100 percent of the injuries produced by exercise. Properly performed exercise can and will go a long way in the direction of preventing injuries. Improperly performed exercise, which usually means sudden movement against resistance, will eventually hurt you.

The above facts apply to every muscle in your body which produces movement and are of particular importance to the muscles of your lower back.

In 1970, in an attempt to solve the problems involved in exercises for this important area of the body, Nautilus introduced the hip and back machine. There are many people walking today who would not be walking if it were not for this machine.

The problems associated with exercises for the lower back, however, were not entirely solved with the hip and back machine. So Nautilus has continued to work on these problems ever since, and the problems have now been solved.

Research with Osteoporosis

The final solution came as a result of an attempt to solve another problem: the problem of providing proper exercise for the muscles of the lower back for people who cannot tolerate even a low level of compression forces on the spine, people suffering the effects of osteoporosis, demineralization of the bones.

Nautilus is now providing the entire funding, in excess of $3 million, for a ten-year research program which is being conducted in cooperation with the School of Medicine at the University of Florida. The purpose of the study is to help determine the effects of exercise for the purpose of preventing osteoporosis or for the rehabilitation of people suffering the effects of osteoporosis.

It now appears that exercise is perhaps the single most important factor required for either the prevention or the treatment of osteoporosis, a condition that affects literally tens of millions of people in this country, particularly older women.

But the Nautilus lower back machine is not only for women who are prone to osteoporosis, it is for literally everyone. Bodybuilders, especially, have a desire for well-developed lower back muscles. And bodybuilders and other athletes need the strength and protection that thick lower back muscles provide during all movement activities.

It is Arthur Jones's opinion that the Nautilus lower back machine is the most important machine that he has ever produced.

Performing the Lower Back Machine

The lower back machine should be used as shown in the following illustrations.

1. Enter machine by straddling seat bottom. Sit forward in seat. Make sure that back is underneath highest roller pad.
2. Stabilize lower body by moving thighs under roller pads. Adjust pads until thighs are secure.
3. Place feet firmly on platform or step.
4. Fasten seat belt.

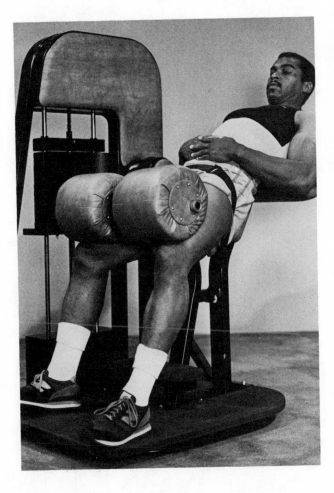

5. Interlace fingers across waist.
6. Move torso backward smoothly and slowly until it is in line with thighs.
7. Pause in contracted position. Do not try to arch back excessively.

8. Return slowly to starting position and repeat. *(Photos by Lewis Green)*

RESISTANCE CURVES OF THE STIFF-LEGGED DEADLIFT AND BACK EXTENSION

The curve of resistance provided by the stiff-legged deadlift starts high and ends low. Assuming a barbell weight of 100 pounds, with no consideration for the body mass of the individual performing the exercise, and assuming a movement of 90 degrees rotating around the axis of the hips while maintaining stiff legs and a flat back, the resistance would be 100 pounds at the start of the upwards movement and zero at the end of the movement. Additional resistance would of course be provided by the body mass of the person performing the exercise, but would vary in the same manner. And, at the end of the movement, in the upright position, 100% of the resistance would be exerting compression forces on the spine while providing no resistance at all for the muscles of the lower back.

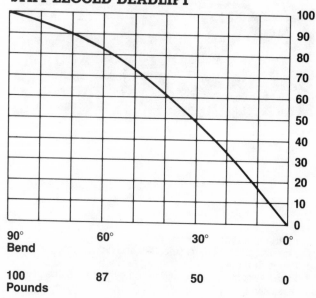

STIFF-LEGGED DEADLIFT

90° Bend	60°	30°	0°
100 Pounds	87	50	0

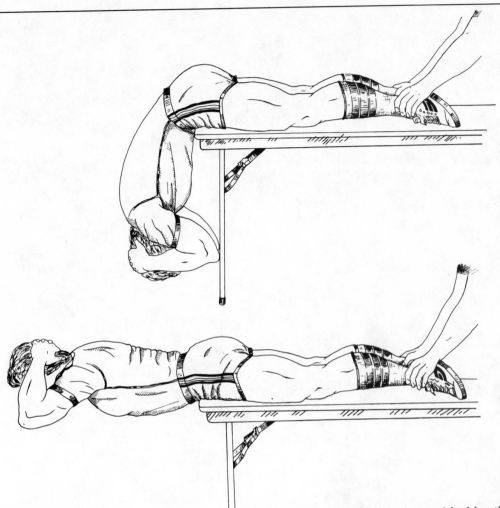

BACK EXTENSION

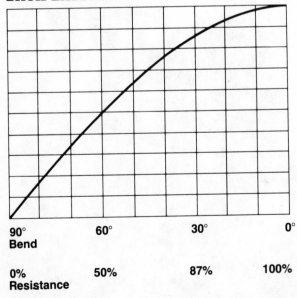

90° Bend	60°	30°	0°
0% Resistance	50%	87%	100%

The curve of resistance provided by the back extension starts low and ends high. This produces a curve that is opposite to that provided by the stiff-legged deadlift. Assuming that the exercise is performed using only the body mass of the individual as a source of resistance, and assuming that a range of movement of 90 degrees is involved, rotating around the axis of the hips with the back being maintained in a straight line, then no resistance is provided at the start of the upward movement while maximum resistance is provided at the end of the movement.

In marked contrast to both the stiff-legged deadlift and back extension, the Nautilus lower back machine provides proper resistance throughout the entire movement. The lower back machine provides a greater range of movement, while removing the compression forces that are involved in the stiff-legged deadlift, and without requiring the hyperextension that is normally suggested in the other exercise.

CHAPTER 9
SUPER-SLOW TRAINING

Fast or slow. Smooth or jerky.
The way you perform each repetition of an exercise is one of the most important factors in successful bodybuilding.

Most bodybuilders perform their repetitions too fast and too jerkily. Fast, jerky repetitions do not effectively isolate individual muscle groups, and proper isolation is important in complete muscular development. Furthermore, fast repetitions transfer much of the resistance away from the muscles to the joints and connective tissues. Not only is this an unproductive way to build muscle, it is dangerous.

Move slower, never faster, if in doubt about the speed of movement on each repetition. This is one of the basic Nautilus training principles. Yet it is also one of the first that is violated by most trainees. It is violated because it is *easier* to move fast and jerkily than it is to move slowly and smoothly. Slow, smooth repetitions soon become a painful, fatiguing experience. Yes, they are painful. But they are very productive.

If your Nautilus exercise has degenerated into a series of fast and jerky repetitions, then you need to try super-slow training. Or if you're at a plateau with your present routine, then super-slow training may be just the change-of-pace program you've been looking for.

Basic Guidelines

Super-slow training on Nautilus equipment applies a positive contraction of 10 seconds and a negative contraction of 4 seconds. In other words, lift the weight in approximately 10 seconds, then lower it to the beginning position in 4 seconds.

At the beginning, you should use a helper with a stopwatch to count the time on each repetition. Ask yourself, "How slowly can I move, yet not stop?" Let's consider this in two different Nautilus machines, the leg extension and the pullover.

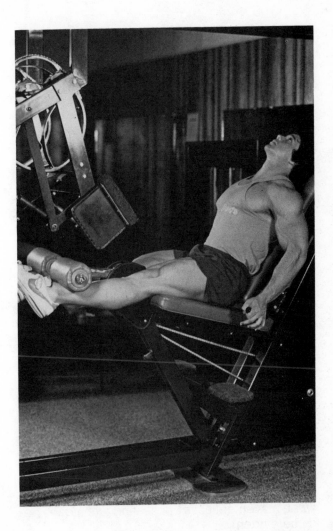

The leg extension is an excellent machine to perform in a super-slow manner. Remember to take 10 seconds in the positive movement and 4 seconds in the negative movement. *(Photo by Ken Neely)*

Super-slow training requires a 10-second positive movement. *(Photo by Lewis Green)*

Performing the Leg Extension

Sit in the proper position with your ankles behind the roller pads. Try to just break the weight stack—barely start to move the resistance. You may move it only a perceptible ⅛ inch. The less you move it, the more control you demonstrate.

Once started, then slow down. Continue to straighten the legs and arrive at the fully extended position at about the 10-second mark.

If you do not perfectly hit 10 seconds, do not be overly concerned. Just aim for 10. Any duration between 8 and 12 seconds is acceptable, but aim for 10. Do not suddenly speed up at the end of the movement merely because you believe your movement is too slow.

Deliberately pause in the contracted position. Then ease out of it gradually. Smoothly increase speed, but still move slowly, and return to the starting position in about 4 seconds.

Feel the weight stack touch, but do not let the slack out of the chain or rest. You want to touch, then barely move again in the positive direction. Start the next repetition immediately but slowly.

Once the resistance becomes difficult, you will tend to alternately stop and heave into the resistance. Try to avoid this. Keep the movement arm traveling at a near constant speed. When it appears that further movement is impossible without compromise of form, failure is attained.

Judge resistance increases with the stopwatch. Once a set begins, start the clock. Stop the clock when movement halts or cheating techniques become evident.

The selected resistance should permit you to perform an exercise for at least 30 seconds. This generally works out to be about two repetitions.

Once you can perform over 70 seconds (4-5 repetitions) without compromising form, a resistance increase is indicated for the next workout.

Women also can get dramatic results from training slowly. *(Photo by Ellington Darden)*

Performing the Pullover

Enter the machine in the usual fashion. Allow the movement arm to pull your shoulders into a stretched position. This is the beginning of the exercise. Start the stopwatch here.

Squeeze the elbows against the upholstery. Steadily increase the force until movement occurs. Proceed very slowly. Do not allow momentum to develop at any point along the range. The entire positive movement should require about 10 seconds.

Pause in the contracted position. Then ease out of the contracted position, slightly increasing the speed. Maintain smoothness. As the stretch is again encountered, move cautiously. Stretch slowly. This, the negative phase of the exercise, should require about 4 seconds.

Begin the next repetition.

Note that the first 15-30 degrees of movement occur quickly. This is common even though the average velocity of the entire movement is acceptably slow.

Almost all momentum can be eliminated from such an exercise. But this requires a little practice. You must develop a feel for how fast you move off the mark. The following mental picture may help.

Mental Practice

Sit in the pullover machine. Assume the stretched position. Pretend that the required force to move the movement arm is 100 pounds. With no intention to move, start to pull slightly with the involved muscles. Pretend that your muscles are pulling with only 5 pounds of force. Nothing happens. No movement occurs.

Increase the force to 10 pounds. Then 20. Then 30. Then 50. Then 75. Then 90. Then 100. Still, no movement occurs.

Then apply 101 pounds of force. The machine begins to move. Until now, the pads have compressed, and the body has slightly contorted, but no movement of the machine has occurred.

But with 101 pounds of force, slight acceleration occurs and the machine moves.

Of course, this entire mental picture is applied in a time frame of approximately a second. The essence of the idea is a gradual buildup of force, as opposed to a sudden one.

Have you ever waited at a rail crossing while a long train stopped and then proceeded? Do you remember the characteristic clatter that moved down the full length of the train as it started? And did you notice that the caboose started to move forward long after the engine was already in motion?

There is a certain amount of unavoidable play in the coupling arms on each train car. If the couplers are pulling, this play is totally eliminated. If they are pushing, the play is as wide as it can be.

When the train stops, the play often widens. Then as it starts, the play is removed. That loud clatter heard is the result of a tremendous force imparted to each successive coupler as the train accelerates forward. Acceleration of the train generally occurs very smoothly and slowly. On close inspection, this slow, smooth acceleration is actually a series of sudden and violent accelerations.

The play in each coupler represents slack in the system between the front and rear ends of the train. The caboose will begin to move forward only after all of that slack is removed.

Pretend that your muscle-joint system is an accelerating train. And pretend that you are going to accelerate your train in such a fashion that the couplers make no noise. To do this you must start each repetition of an exercise ever so gradually. Consider this concept as you begin the positive phase of each repetition of an exercise. You will provide more exercise to that part of the muscle's function, and forces will be minimized even further.

Boyer Coe demonstrates a super-slow, positive movement on the behind-neck pulldown. The positive movement should take approximately 10 seconds to complete.

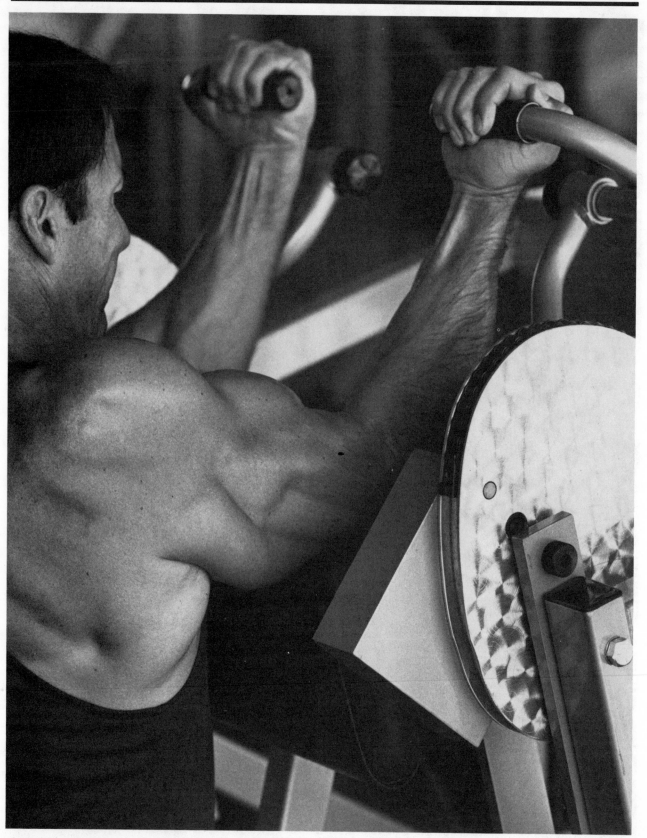

Super-slow repetitions intensify the stress placed on the involved muscles.

Advantages of Slow Training

Q. *What are the advantages of super-slow training?*

A. Super-slow training serves as the best means to correct poor form in any exercise involving positive contraction. It eliminates momentum, making efficient use of the Nautilus cam. It also serves to isolate those glossed-over points in your range of motion where you habitually, and otherwise undetectably, shift, shrug, lunge, heave, and invoke other muscles to complete the movement. These weak areas are better addressed, since you are more aware of each position of possible motion, and reliance on momentum is restricted. For the same reasons, the exercise is safer because of lowered forces.

Disadvantages

Q. *What are the disadvantages of super-slow exercise?*

A. Super-slow exercise may prove boring to some. The intensity of contraction may prove to be too uncomfortable, also. It's not an easy or fun way to train. Exercise is most efficient, however, when it is most difficult and least fun. Super-slow exercise is very effective and beneficially so. And tangible benefits often serve to motivate the most discouraged trainee.

Slow training may prove cumbersome in a commercial facility. Done well, it often requires an instructor with a stopwatch. But with a little practice, the stopwatch can be discarded. The repetition scheme already outlined will suffice.

Selecting the Resistance

Q. *Based on my previous training experience, how do I judge the resistance with which to begin a super-slow program?*

A. You will need less resistance in the beginning. But you may soon need heavier resistance in the same exercises as you once performed them

in the conventional manner. The first few workouts may require some experimentation.

Reduce the resistance used in the conventional manner by about 30 percent. This deliberately underestimates the resistance that you probably need, but it allows you to begin with strict form as you discover your actual requirements. Increase the resistance in each exercise by 2.5 or 1.25 pounds until perfect form permits approximately 70 seconds of work.

Duration

Q. *Doesn't super-slow training take longer to perform than the basic lift-in-2-seconds, lower-in-4-seconds approach?*

A. No. Super-slow training requires the same time allotted to the set and the complete workout as the basic method. The common repetition scheme of 8-12 repetitions, up-2-seconds, down-4-seconds, represents a window of time to achieve momentary muscular failure in approximately 70 seconds. This is the same time frame we strive for in the super-slow application.

Application to Compound Movements

Q. *Can this style of training be applied to compound movements that involve more than one joint, or is it strictly limited to single-joint, rotational movements?*

A. Super-slow training can be applied to all exercises, even those that involve compound movements. Care must be taken in compound movements, however, to avoid or minimize the time spent in a position of infinite moment arm. This is a position where an extremity's bones are aligned so that effective resistance is zero. It is a common problem encountered in exercises such as a chinup or pulldown.

For example: Start the pulldown movement by slightly bending the arms. If you are not careful, you will move the first few degrees so suddenly that your extended arms encounter no real work. Then on the return, go all the way to the straight position. But move immediately and slowly out of this position. If you linger in this position, the intensity of the exercise is compromised.

Cardiovascular Effects

Q. *Is it true that super-slow exercise has less effect on the cardiovascular-pulmonary system than the conventional repetition scheme?*

A. No. Eventually, once the correct resistance levels are established, super-slow exercise provides the same marked heart/lung effect as other valid approaches utilizing Nautilus machines.

Negative Application

Q. *The basic Nautilus guidelines suggest that the lowering portion of the exercise be performed half as fast as the lifting phase. Why does the lowering part of the super-slow approach remain at 4 seconds?*

A. Since super-slow training requires such slow movement, the resistance levels are markedly reduced. The quality of the back pressure involved during the lowering portion of the exercise is also reduced. If we move slower than a rate of 4 seconds, negative work during this phase is reduced even further because of our ability to partially rest. In other words, going slower means easier—exactly opposite to our intensity requirements.

Also, simply dropping the resistance makes the work easier. Therefore, keep the rate of movement during the lowering phase ´the same as before.

Q. *If the quality of negative work provided during the lowering phase of the exercise is reduced, is negative work less important in the super-slow application?*

A. No. It merely appears that its significance is lessened. Negative work is just as important in the super-slow method as before. Indeed, it is even more important.

Without the back pressure of negative work, you would be able to move positively, then rest, then continue positively again. Negative work potential is crucially important during the lifting portion of super-slow training. It is invaluable for maintaining high-intensity work.

Great for Bodybuilding

Q. *How should an advanced bodybuilder use super-slow training?*

A. Super-slow training is tailor-made for bodybuilding because it allows you to isolate a muscle group better than normal training does. Effective muscle isolation leads to better and more complete development.

Initially, you should experiment with super-slow training during several workouts. It will take at least two sessions to learn the skill of moving slowly on each repetition. Once you have mastered the skill, there are two basic ways that you can use super-slow training.

One, use it on all of your exercises as a change of pace for two weeks in a row. Then go back to your normal workout for the next three months and try it again.

Two, use it selectively on Nautilus machines that you have reached a plateau on. For example, suppose you've been stuck on the leg curl with 120 pounds for the last month. You cannot do more than 10 repetitions in the normal fashion with that weight. So, you reduce the resistance and try super-slow leg curls for three consecutive training sessions. That should promptly help you to break out of your training slump on the leg curl. You should now be able to perform at least 12 repetitions with 120 pounds. The same concept can be applied to any Nautilus machine.

Super-slow training works well with multiple-joint movements such as the overhead press.

CHAPTER 10
ADVANCED BODYBUILDING PRINCIPLES

Twenty-one basic training rules were detailed in *The Nautilus Bodybuilding Book.* All of them apply to advanced bodybuilders, but the following merit review.

1. Perform no more than 12 exercises in any workout. Usually only one set of each exercise is done.

2. Train no more than three times a week. Each workout should involve the entire body, as opposed to splitting the routine into lower and upper body work on separate days.

3. Select resistance for each exercise that allows the performance of between 8 and 12 repetitions.

4. Continue each exercise until no additional repetitions are possible. When 12 or more repetitions can be performed, increase the resistance by approximately 5 percent at the next workout.

5. Position the body correctly on all single-joint rotary machines. The axis of the cam should be in line with the joint of the body part that is being exercised.

6. Keep the body properly aligned on each machine. Avoid twisting or shifting the torso and trunk during the last repetitions.

7. Accentuate the lowering portion of each repetition.

8. Move slower, never faster, if in doubt about the speed of movement.

9. Do everything possible to isolate and work each large muscle group to exhaustion.

10. Relax completely the body parts that are not involved in each exercise. Pay special attention to relaxing the face and hand muscles.

11. Attempt constantly to increase the number of repetitions or the amount of weight, or both. But do not sacrifice form in an attempt to produce results.

12. Train with a partner who can reinforce proper form on each machine.

13. Keep accurate records—date, resistance, repetitions, and overall training time—of each workout.

14. Get ample rest after each training session. High-intensity exercise necessitates a recovery period of at least 48 hours. Muscles grow during rest, not during exercise.

15. Emphasize harder, briefer workouts as progress is made. Reduce the number of exercises from 12 to 10 and the times per week from three to two.

Putting Principles into Practice

After the 1982 Mr. Olympia contest and more than 18 years of competitive bodybuilding, Boyer Coe retired. Following this decision, he took a three-month layoff from training, the longest period of inactivity he had ever experienced.

"I've been competing in bodybuilding contests for almost 20 years," Boyer said, "and I found it a great deal more satisfying in my early years of competition.

"For the last three years, I've entered more contests than any other pro bodybuilder, and probably have experienced more frustration, regardless of whether I won or lost. One of the reasons is that the bodybuilding magazines build you up as some sort of superhero to the general public. If you don't look better at each contest—not the same, but better—then the fans become disappointed and at times actually turn against you. If only the muscle publications would present a more down-to-earth image of the pro bodybuilder! After all, we are only human."

In January of 1983, Coe thought a change was necessary. He left California and moved to Lake Helen, Florida, where he went to work for Arthur Jones and Nautilus Sports/Medical Industries. Jones needed a man to help him publish a new fitness magazine, and Boyer's background qualified him for the job.

Furthermore, both Jones and Coe wanted to see

Mike Mentzer is shown training Boyer Coe at the Nautilus Television Studios. This workout was videotaped with eight synchronous cameras. *(Photo by Ellington Darden)*

Advanced bodybuilders actually need less overall exercise than do beginners.

For six months, every repetition of every exercise performed by Boyer Coe was videotaped with multiple cameras. *(Photo by Ellington Darden)*

Ellington Darden and Boyer Coe.

the effect of brief, high-intensity Nautilus exercise on Coe's body. Together they outlined a year's worth of special Nautilus workouts.

The objective of the training was to get Boyer's body as strong and as lean as possible. Jones would supervise Boyer's workouts, and every repetition of every exercise would be videotaped with eight synchronous cameras: Eventually, edited versions of these tapes would be available to the public.

After a month of trial-and-error experimentation, Jones and Coe settled on two routines that produced very significant results.

Boyer trained three times a week, on a Monday, Wednesday, and Friday schedule. He alternated the following two workouts:

Boyer Coe's Routine A

1. Duo squat
2. Pullover
3. Overhead press
4. Behind neck pulldown
5. 10° chest
6. Abdominal
7. Multi triceps
8. Multi biceps
9. Lower back

Boyer Coe's Routine B

1. Calf raise
2. Leg extension
3. Leg curl
4. Chin
5. Decline press
6. Rowing torso
7. Arm cross
8. Rotary torso
9. 70° shoulder
10. Lateral raise
11. Neck and shoulder

During the first week, Routine A is performed on Monday and Friday. On Wednesday, Routine B is used.

During the second week, Routine B is executed on Monday and Friday and Routine A is used on Wednesday. In other words, both routines are performed three times every two weeks.

Routines A and B are two examples of advanced bodybuilding programs that concentrate on overall development. The majority of your year-round training should involve your major muscle groups at least three times every two weeks.

Using the 15 previously listed principles or rules, you should be able to design numerous productive Nautilus routines.

BOYER COE'S WORKOUT
JUNE 17, 1983

Routine A

1.	Duo squat	460/18
2.	Pullover	210/10
3.	Overhead press	160/8
4.	Behind-neck pulldown	170/10
5.	10° chest	190/9
6.	Abdominal	180/10
7.	Multi triceps	165/7
8.	Multi biceps	120/6
9.	Lower back	245/10

Total training time: 14:06

BOYER COE'S WORKOUT
JUNE 20, 1983

Routine B

1.	Calf raise	350/15
2.	Leg extension	310/9
3.	Leg curl	190/9
4.	Chin	70/7
5.	Decline press	210/7
6.	Rowing torso	150/10
7.	Arm cross	140/11
8.	Rotary torso	210/R12 L12
9.	70° shoulder	170/10
10.	Lateral raise	110/5
11.	Neck and shoulder	100/14

Total training time: 21:48

Specialized Nautilus Routines

Boyer Coe alternated Routine A and Routine B and trained hard three times a week. His strength increased steadily on each exercise. At the end of the fourth month, however, his progress plateaued. Thereafter, instead of training hard three times a week, he began training to momentary muscular failure only twice a week, on Mondays and Fridays. All exercises performed during his Wednesday workouts were stopped two repetitions short of an all-out effort. Reducing the intensity of his Wednesday workout allowed his body additional time to recover. As a result, the plateau was broken and his strength increased weekly as before. Steady improvement continued for two months, then another plateau was reached.

When the second plateau was recognized, Boyer's progress was analyzed. It was decided that a change was necessary. Super-slow, negative-only, and specialized routines were employed to break Boyer's training plateau and shock his body into additional growth.

Sooner or later, if you're an advanced bodybuilder, you'll reach a similar plateau or sticking point in your routine. Or you may simply have certain muscle groups that need special attention. For example, your arms may be lagging behind your torso. Or your chest may require some direct work. Or your calves may be disproportionately small compared to your thighs.

The second section of this book describes and illustrates dozens of specialized Nautilus routines. Many of these routines have been used successfully by Boyer Coe, Mike Mentzer, Ray Mentzer, and other advanced bodybuilders.

PART TWO

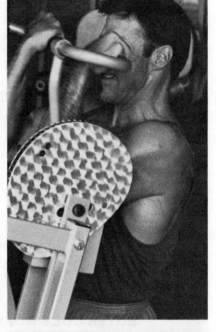

ADVANCED ROUTINES

CHAPTER 11
HOW TO BUILD LATS WIDER THAN YOUR SHOULDERS

How would you like to have lats wider than your shoulders?" Arthur Jones asks a group of interested bodybuilders. "When standing relaxed and viewed from behind, you would actually have latissimus dorsi muscles that are broader than your shoulders are wide.

"Well, it's possible," Jones says. "But in order to develop your lats fully, you must understand and apply certain physiological principles to your training program."

What are these physiological principles? Primarily, they can be grouped into three categories: direct resistance, pre-exhaustion technique, and style of performance. A thorough description of each principle follows.

Direct Resistance

The latissimus dorsi muscles are the largest of the upper body. They join the lower part of the spine and sweep up to the armpits, where they are inserted into the upper arm bones. When the latissimus dorsi muscles contract they pull the upper arms from an overhead position down and around the shoulder axes. This rotational movement can take place with the upper arms in front of or at the sides of the torso.

Arthur Jones understood the physiological functions of the latissimus dorsi, and it was obvious to him that all standard exercises for the lats left much to be desired. Chin-ups, pulldowns, behind-neck chins, pullovers with barbells and dumbbells, and rowing exercises of a wide variety do provide some work for those muscles. But they all have one common fault: They involve the muscles of the arms as well as the muscles of the back.

The latissimus dorsi muscles are attached to and move the upper arms. For direct exercise, the resistance must be applied against the upper arms or elbows. What happens to the forearms is of no importance. A criminal is hanged by suspending his weight from his head, thus imposing

resistance on his neck. If he were hanged by his hair, the hair might pull out before any results were produced in the neck. A similar situation exists in barbell exercises for the latissimus muscles. Instead of applying the resistance directly against the prime body parts, the upper arms, such exercises apply resistance against the hands and forearms. This creates a weak link. You are forced to stop in such an exercise when your arms fail, not when the latissimus muscles become exhausted.

So you are limited in such exercises by the existing strength of your upper arms. Being smaller and weaker than your latissimus muscles, your upper arm muscles fail long before the much larger latissimus muscles have been worked hard enough to induce maximum growth stimulation.

Jones effectively solved the weak-link problem in 1970 when he began manufacturing the Nautilus pullover and behind-neck machines. Although many companies have tried to copy Jones's equipment, none has been as successful as Nautilus in making efficient direct-resistance machines. Unfortunately, few bodybuilders have ever used the Nautilus pullover and behind-neck machines in the correct manner. That manner, which pays special attention to smooth, slow movements, will be described later in this chapter.

Pre-Exhaustion Technique

Solving the weak-link problem also opened Jones's eyes to the pre-exhaustion technique. The purpose of the pre-exhaustion technique is to fatigue momentarily a body part by performing a single-joint exercise that isolates a specific muscle. This is immediately followed by a multiple-joint exercise that brings into action other surrounding muscles to force the pre-exhausted muscle to work even harder.

Jones knew that in order to link the latissimus muscles with the biceps muscles, several com-

The outstanding back development of Tony Pearson.

bination torso and arm exercises were required. Trial-and-error research proved to him that pulldowns, behind-neck exercises, and chins or negative chins should be performed immediately after the Nautilus pullover or behind-neck machines. When a pulling movement for the biceps and torso is performed after a direct exercise for the lats, the biceps are temporarily stronger than the pre-exhausted lats. Thus a trainee can use his biceps to work his latissimus muscles much harder than would otherwise be possible.

Style of Performance

A force plate is a delicate measuring device that can be connected to an oscilloscope. Accurate measurements of force during a barbell exercise can be recorded by standing on the plate as you perform an exercise. The difference between the performance of fast and slow repetitions, as recorded on the screen, is dramatic.

Fast repetitions produce peaks and drops on the oscilloscope. These peaks and drops indicate that a 100-pound barbell, while being lifted, can exert from more than 500 pounds of force to less than zero. Such erratic force is not only unproductive as far as muscle stimulation is concerned, but also very dangerous to the joints, muscles, and connective tissues.

Slow, steady repetitions produce a relatively smooth tracing on the oscilloscope. This kind of tracing indicates that the barbell's resistance is being directed properly against the muscle throughout the exercise's range of movement.

Jones found slow repetitions performed with a barbell or Nautilus machine to be much more productive than fast repetitions for bodybuilding. As a general rule, you should move slow enough to remove the influence of momentum from the exercise. If in doubt about your speed of movement, always move slower.

Most bodybuilders are aware of the importance of chosing exercises that isolate specific muscle groups as much as possible. What many may not be aware of, however, is that isolation of a particular muscle is directly related to ability to relax the uninvolved muscles.

If you perform the Nautilus pullover machine for the latissimus dorsi muscles, it is to your advantage to relax your legs, arms, hands, neck, and face. Gripping with the hands involves many muscles of the forearms and upper arms. Moving the torso forward or sideways brings into action the abdominals or obliques. Moving the head works the neck. Even tensing the jaws, squinting the eyes, groaning, or yelling during the latter repetitions can weaken the neurological input to the lats.

Your intention in performing on the pullover machine is to build muscular size and strength in the latissimus dorsi muscles. Learning to relax all other muscles while slowly contracting the lats will help stimulate the maximum number of muscle fibers.

A slow style of performance, with special emphasis on relaxation of the uninvolved muscles, should be used for more efficient results on all your bodybuilding exercises.

The Lat Routine

Five Nautilus machine exercises make up this special latissimus dorsi cycle.
1. Behind neck
2. Pullover
3. Behind-neck pulldown
4. Rowing torso
5. Chin, negative only

The exercises should be performed in the above order, with little rest between sets. Each exercise should immediately follow the preceding one. Each set should be carried to the point of momentary muscular failure, which failure should usually occur between 8 and 12 repetitions.

For best possible results, only one set of each of

the five exercises should be performed during your workout. The entire cycle for the lats should take less than seven minutes. That's right, seven minutes. And this routine should not be repeated more often than twice a week for two consecutive weeks. You may repeat the program every four months. Quality, not quantity, is important in working the lats. Let's carefully examine the quality way to perform each exercise.

Behind neck: This machine provides direct, rotary resistance for one of the primary functions of the lats. Be sure that the seat is adjusted so that your shoulder joints are in line with the axes of the cams. Place your upper arms between the roller pads. Move both arms downward until the roller pads touch your torso. It is important to keep the roller pads on the triceps area during the exercise. Do not allow the upper arms and forearms to rotate forward. This brings the pectoral muscles into the exercise. Return slowly to the crossed-arm position behind your neck and repeat. When you can no longer move your upper arms into the fully contracted position with your elbows next to your torso, stop the exercise. Immediately get out of the machine and run to the pullover.

Pullover: The Nautilus pullover is the best overall latissimus exercise ever devised. Performed after the behind-neck machine, the pullover will cause your lats to burn with an intensity that you must experience to believe. The seat should be adjusted so that your shoulder joints are in line with the axes of the cams. With the aid of the foot pedal, place your elbows on the pads of the movement arm. Your hands should be open and resting on the curved portion of the bar. Slowly rotate your elbows as far back as possible. This provides maximum stretch for your latissimus muscles. Rotate your elbows downward in a smooth, nonjerky fashion until the handbar touches your waist. Pause and contract your lats as hard as possible. Return slowly to the stretched position and repeat

until exhausted. Remember, it is important to isolate your lats by relaxing the surrounding muscles. Do not grip the bar with your hands, lean your head and torso forward, or move your hips and legs. After the final repetition of the pullover, instantly belt yourself into the torso arm machine and perform behind-neck pulldowns.

Behind-neck pulldown: The behind-neck pulldown employs a parallel grip, instead of the traditional pronated or palms-down grip. A parallel grip places the biceps into the position of greatest strength. Thus, while the ability to work the lats will still be limited by the strength of the biceps, this limitation will be reduced as much as possible. Furthermore, if you perform the pulldown after exercising on the behind-neck and pullover machines, your biceps will temporarily be stronger than your latissimus muscles. Your biceps can now force your lats to a deeper state of muscular exhaustion. Perform as many smooth, slow behind-neck pulldowns as you can. After several repetitions, because of the muscular pain, you'll want to make terrible faces, grit your teeth, and twist from side to side. Try to keep such behavior to a bare minimum and you'll get much better results.

Rowing torso: This machine provides direct exercise for many small muscles that surround the lats, such as the rhomboid, trapezius, infraspinatus, and posterior deltoid. The rowing torso also provides a temporary rest for the lats and biceps, which will be involved once again on the next exercise. Enter the machine with your back toward the weight stack. Place your arms between the roller pads. Move your arms in a rowing fashion as far back as possible. Be sure to keep your hands, elbows, and shoulders parallel to the floor during the entire range of movement. Pause in the contracted position. Return slowly to the starting position and repeat. After the last repetition, move quickly to the final exercise:

Behind neck: Keep your triceps on the roller pads throughout the movement. Do not let your arms rotate forward.

Pullover: Make your lats do the work. Pull with your elbows, not your hands.

Behind-neck pulldown: Lean forward and bring the bar smoothly behind your neck.

Rowing torso: Keep your elbows and hands at shoulder level during all repetitions.

The thick, muscular backs of Johnny Fuller and Robby Robinson.

negative chins.

Chin, negative only: This final exercise adds the finishing touch to your lats. And believe me, at the completion of 10 correct repetitions, your lats will be finished. The negative chin is best executed on the Nautilus multi-exercise machine. Depending on your strength level, you may or may not need to add the weight-belt attachment around your hips. In the negative chin, you will be concentrating on the lowering portion only of the traditional chinning movement. Using the steps of the multi-exercise machine, quickly climb to the top position until your chin is over the crossbar. Bend your knees and lower your body to the slow count of 8. Do as many 8-second repetitions as possible, usually 2 or 3. Do several more in the 6-second range, then more in the 5-second and 4-second range. After each repetition, climb quickly to the top position. When you can no longer control your lowering movement, stop the exercise.

That's it: one set of five exercises for your lats. Five exercises that take a total training time of less than seven minutes. But during that seven minutes it will seem as if all the blood in your body is being directed toward your lats. Such a program will work your lats almost literally "into the ground" from every possible angle, over the entire range of movement, from several different directions.

What to Expect

If these five exercises fail to produce at least three times the rate of progress you have experienced from your previous lat routine, then you are not performing them correctly. Or you may not be working hard enough, or you may be pausing between exercises. Performed properly, these exercises are capable of producing as much as ten times the results usually produced by conventional training methods, at least as far as the return of results in proportion to expenditure of energy is

Chin, negative only: Climb the stairs quickly, get your chin over the bar, and lower slowly.

concerned.

"The potential size of the lats," Arthur Jones says, "is so great that they are capable of attaining a size far out of proportion to the maximum potential size of any other human muscular structure. So don't be surprised when you start seeing men with lats so big that they defy belief."

Would you like lats wider than your shoulders? Apply the Nautilus principles to your training program and you won't be disappointed.

Nautilus Lat Routine

Date						
Behind neck						
Pullover						
Behind-neck pulldown						
Rowing						
Chin, negative only						

CHAPTER 12
FOR A DEEP, THICK CHEST

On February 24, 1983, an interesting discussion took place at Nautilus Sports/Medical Industries in Lake Helen, Florida. Most of the conversation was between Arthur Jones and Vic Tanny, Sr. Jones had trained at Tanny's gym in Santa Monica for several months in 1947. Others present were Mike and Ray Mentzer, Boyer Coe, and Ellington Darden.

"You know," Arthur said, "there were some big guys training in California in 1947. I remember Clancy Ross. He had a huge upper body with unusually large and muscular pecs.

"The fact that there were a few bodybuilders back then that tried this feat will let you know something about the thickness of their pectoral development. Ross, John Farbotnik, and George Eiferman would be cooling off after a workout. They'd lean forward, place a 10-pound barbell plate between their pecs, contract, and try to hold it in place. I never saw or heard of any of them actually succeeding. But just that they would even think of trying it is an indication of their pec thickness."

"What was the reason behind their deep, thick chest development?" Mike Mentzer asked. "Did they do anything special?"

"I think much of it," Jones answered, "was related to their strength. They were damned strong. They weren't afraid to handle heavy poundages in their upper body exercises. And they didn't train for four hours a day, seven days a week. They trained heavy and they trained briefly."

"Yeah, I can still see Clancy Ross," Tanny said, "doing incline presses with 165-pound dumbbells in each hand. You certainly don't do many sets with that kind of iron, do you?"

Heavy, but brief, exercise, once again, is the key to building massive muscles. As a result of simple trial-and-error experimentation, most of the old-timers trained this way. Unlike today's bodybuilders, they weren't subjected to all the

An unusual display of upper body mass by Samir Bannout.

Bertil Fox, according to one Mr. Olympia judge, has the thickest pectorals in professional bodybuilding.

glossy four-color muscle magazines' marathon routines to lead them in the opposite direction.

"Jones is right," said a judge of the 1982 Mr. Olympia contest, who read this chapter prior to publication. "There wasn't a single competitor in last year's Mr. Olympia who had really thick pecs. Chris Dickerson didn't. And neither did Frank Zane. Bertil Fox had the thickest chest in the contest, but he still couldn't hold a 10-pound plate between his pecs."

If a deep, thick chest is your goal, the following three chest routines are what the old timers would prescribe.

Chest Routine 1

This routine uses the pre-exhaustion technique to fatigue the pectoral muscles thoroughly. Three exercises are performed in this order:

1. Decline press, immediately followed by
2. Arm cross, immediately followed by
3. Dip, negative only

Decline press: Normally, on the double chest machine, the decline press is performed after the arm cross. In this double pre-exhaustion routine, however, the decline press is done first. Performing it first, instead of second, you should be able to use approximately 20 additional pounds. Keep your elbows high throughout the movement and try to perform 8 to 12 repetitions in good form. Avoid arching your back on the last repetitions.

When you can no longer complete a repetition, lower the weight with the foot pedal. Quickly, have an assistant reduce the weight two or three plates and immediately get your forearms into position for the arm cross.

Arm cross: Push with your forearms, not your hands, as you smoothly bring both elbows to the contracted position in front of your chest. Keep your head against the back pad. Do not try to lean forward in the contracted position. Return to the stretched position, with your elbows behind your shoulders, and repeat for 8 to 12 repetitions.

Get out of the double chest and run to the multi-exercise machine for the dip.

Dip, negative only: The decline press and the arm cross should have very thoroughly pre-exhausted your pectoral muscles. The dip will bring into action your triceps to force your pectorals to a much deeper level of exhaustion.

Make sure that the carriage on the multi-exercise machine is adjusted beforehand to the correct height. The dip bars should be high enough to provide maximum stretch in the bottom position.

Most bodybuilders will need extra resistance added to their bodyweight to get the best results from negative-only dips. This is easily accomplished on the multi-exercise machine by using the padded waist belt attached to the movement arm.

To perform negative-only dips, step into the belt and adjust it securely around your hips. Climb the stairs until your arms are straight. Bend your knees, stabilize yourself, and lower slowly by bending your arms to the stretched position. This lowering movement should take at least eight seconds. Quickly, climb back to the top and repeat for 8 to 12 repetitions.

It is very important in negative-only dips to stretch fully in the bottom position, climb as fast as possible back to the straight-armed position, and lower your body smoothly under control during each repetition.

Decline press: Keep your elbows wide.

Dip, negative only: Use your legs to get into the top position. Lower slowly and repeat.

Arm cross: Make your pectorals work by pushing with your forearms, not your hands.

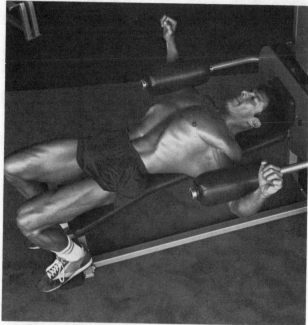

40° chest/shoulder: Contract your pectorals intensely at the top position.

10° chest: Concentrate on stretching and contracting your pectorals during each repetition.

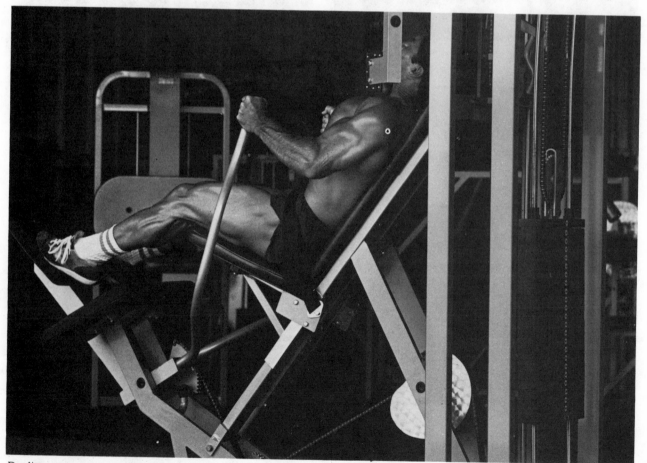

Decline press, negative only: Leg-press the foot pedal and lower slowly with your arms.

Chest Routine 2

Chest Routine 2 is similar to Routine 1. But instead of having a single-joint movement between two multiple-joint movements, Routine 2 has a multiple-joint movement between two single-joint movements. Again, three Nautilus exercises are performed back-to-back:

1. 40° chest/shoulder, immediately followed by
2. Decline press, negative only, immediately followed by
3. 10° chest

40° chest/shoulder: Adjust the seat bottom so the tops of your shoulders are in line with the axes of the cams. Place your arms under the roller pads. The pads should be in the crooks of your elbows. Move both arms in a rotary fashion until the roller pads touch over your shoulders. Pause. Lower slowly to the stretched position and repeat for 8 to 12 repetitions. Instantly go to the double chest machine.

Decline press, negative only: For this exercise, you'll need to use at least 40 percent more resistance than you'd normally handle. Perform the positive part of the exercise with your legs by using the foot pedal. Remove your legs and lower slowly with your arms until a full stretch is felt across your chest. Take at least 8 seconds to lower the movement arms. Place both feet on the foot pedal and press until your arms are straight. Repeat the slow lowering process for 8 to 12 repetitions. Move quickly to the 10° chest machine.

10° chest: Lie on your back with your head higher than your hips. Place your arms under the roller pads. The pads should be in the crooks of your elbows. Move both arms in a rotary fashion until the roller pads touch over your chest. Pause in the contracted position. Lower slowly to the starting position and repeat for 8 to 12 repetitions.

Mike Mentzer's Chest Routine

Mike Mentzer's pectorals have frequently lagged behind his other torso muscles. Prior to his 1983 seminar tour of Europe, Mike used Chest Routine 2 for several weeks.

"This routine really hits the pecs," Mike says. "In just two weeks my chest responded more than it ever has before."

Here's a listing of the weight and repetitions that Mike used for his chest on July 20, 1983:

Chest Routine 2

1. 40° chest/shoulder	300/6
2. Decline press, negative only	325/10
3. 10° chest	275/8

Chest Routine 3

Chest Routine 3 concentrates primarily on stretching and deepening the rib cage. It involves the following three exercises:

1. Pullover, negative only, immediately followed by
2. Pullover, immediately followed by
3. 70° shoulder

Pullover, negative only: Increase the resistance approximately 40 percent above what you would handle in the normal, positive-negative fashion. You'll need one or two helpers to assist you in doing the positive portion of the pullover in moving the bar into the fully contracted position. It is important that your assistants make the transfer smoothly to your arms. Pause in the fully contracted position and rotate your arms slowly to the stretched position. The slow arm rotation should take at least 8 seconds. On your verbal cue, the assistants should grasp the movement arm and bring it down to the contracted position. Repeat the slow lowering for 8 to 12 repetitions.

By the end of this set, your back and chest should be burning. Your breathing should be heavy and your rib cage should feel significantly expanded.

You are now ready to begin a new set of normal, positive-negative pullovers. But first, one of the assistants should reduce the weight by approximately 50 percent.

Pullover: On the pullover, it is important to emphasize deep, forceful breathing on both the negative and positive movements. Try to expand your rib cage fully on each breath. Stretch as much as you can in the extended position by moving slowly and relaxing gradually. Perform 8 to 12 slow, stretching repetitions.

70° shoulder: This new machine provides great exercise for the tie-in among the deltoids, pectorals, and rib cage. Adjust the seat so the tops of your shoulders are in line with the axes of the cams. Place your arms under the roller pads. The pads should be in the crooks of your elbows. Extend your head and rest it on the pad behind your shoulders. You should be looking at the ceiling. Move both arms in a rotary fashion until the roller pads touch. Pause. Lower slowly to the stretched position and repeat for 8 to 12 repetitions.

Using the Chest Routines

The suggested use of the three chest routines is as follows: Perform Routine 1 on Monday and Routine 2 on Friday. On Wednesday, use Routine 3. Do the routine first in your workout and limit your total exercises for that day to ten or fewer. Perform the appropriate routine on Monday, Wednesday, and Friday for two consecutive weeks. Go back to your normal workouts for at least three months. If your chest needs additional specialization, you may return to the suggested routines for two weeks every three or four months.

And remember, for a deeper and thicker chest, train heavier and train briefer.

Pullover, negative only: Don't be afraid to work heavy on this productive exercise.

Pullover: Resist the temptation to lean forward excessively in the contracted position.

Nautilus Chest Routines

ROUTINE 1

Date						
Decline press						
Arm cross						
Dip, negative only						

ROUTINE 2

Date						
40° chest/shoulder						
Decline press, negative only						
10° chest						

ROUTINE 3

Date						
Pullover, negative only						
Pullover						
70° shoulder						

70° shoulder: Force the pads together by contracting your pectorals and deltoids.

CHAPTER 13
SHOULDERS
MAKE THE MAN

Two-foot-wide shoulders," Arthur Jones says, "are as rare as hen's teeth. The only man I ever saw with shoulders 24 inches wide was Bill Trumbo. Trumbo was training at Vic Tanny's gym in 1947. Every time I saw those shoulders I had to stop and shake my head in amazement."

Nothing sets a man off from his peers quite like broad shoulders. "Shoulders make the man" is still a commonly used expression among hard-working men. No competitive bodybuilder has ever been criticized for having shoulders too wide.

But in 1947, according to Arthur Jones and Vic Tanny, there were a few bodybuilders who showed up in the audience at various California physique contests with shoulders that were indeed too wide—too wide to be true!

What these bodybuilders would do was wear as many as seven specially tailored sweaters. The first one would have an extra-large neck hole, a bottom that stopped at the mid-torso, and sleeves that ended just past the elbows. Each additional sweater would have a slightly smaller neck hole and a slightly longer bottom and longer sleeves. The final sweater would be very large through the shoulders, chest, and upper arms, but fit in the normal fashion at the neck, waist, and wrist.

At first glance, you thought such guys had unbelievably large shoulders and arms. Next, you figured it must be a joke. Finally, you realized that these guys were serious, dead serious.

If shoulders make the man, then these guys, for perhaps the first time in their lives, were real men. At least they were in their own imaginations with all their sweaters in place.

Real-man shoulders, however, are not made from wool, but from muscle. And muscle grows from lifting iron, not lifting sweaters.

The ideal physique would have all major muscle groups maximally, yet symmetrically, developed. The elusive ultimate physique, someone

Dennis Tinerino's shoulders are among the broadest in bodybuilding.

The striated shoulders of Boyer Coe. *(Photo by John Balik)*

once said, would go one step further by the over-development of the deltoids.

If the ultimate physique is your goal, the following routine is a long step in that direction.

A Super-Slow Breakdown Routine for the Shoulders

This shoulder routine concentrates on the middle deltoid, which raises the upper arm sideways. When fully developed, the middle deltoid adds width and mass to the shoulders.

The deltoids respond very well to super-slow training. And because of the construction of deltoid muscle, the shoulders lend themselves to breakdown training.

Breakdown training involves working to exhaustion with a given weight and quickly reducing the resistance and working to failure again. Usually, the weight is decreased twice and three consecutive sets of the same exercise are performed.

The best exercise for the middle deltoid is the lateral raise performed on the new Nautilus lateral raise machine. The primary movement on the double shoulder machine may be used in place of the new machine. The two machines function in a similar manner.

Three descending sets are performed in the super-slow manner:

1. Lateral raise to momentary exhaustion; decrease the resistance by 20 percent
2. Lateral raise to momentary exhaustion; decrease the resistance by another 20 percent
3. Lateral raise to momentary exhaustion

Super-slow set 1: On super-slow training you'll need to start with approximately 30 percent less resistance than you normally use. Adjust the seat so that your shoulder joints are in line with the axes of the cams. Grasp the handles lightly and pull back. Make sure your elbows are slightly behind your torso and firmly against the movement arms.

Lift your elbows and upper arms very slowly, inch by inch, until they are about ear level. Take 10 seconds for this slow, positive movement. Pause briefly in the contracted position. Lower smoothly in 4 seconds to the bottom position. Start the next repetition immediately but slowly. Continue until momentary muscular exhaustion, which exhaustion should occur after 4 or 5 super-slow repetitions.

Have an assistant decrease the resistance by approximately 20 percent (usually two plates) and begin set 2.

Super-slow set 2: Lift your elbows and upper arms, once again, very slowly to ear level. Pause. Lower smoothly and repeat for 4 or 5 repetitions. Try to adhere to the 10-second positive and 4-second negative count on each repetition.

For the best results, emphasize perfect form on all repetitions. Avoid arching your back, moving your head, or twisting from side to side. Keep your facial expressions and teeth gritting to a bare minimum. Concentrate intensely on isolating your deltoids and relax, as best you can, all your uninvolved muscles.

Decrease the resistance for the second time by another 20 percent or two plates. Your deltoids will be in torture as you start set 3.

Super-slow set 3: Follow the same procedure as before. Lift slowly and lower smoothly for 4 or 5 repetitions. On the final repetition, your deltoids should be ready to explode. If you want the ultimate physique, however, one further set should be done.

At the end of your final super-slow repetition, without reducing the weight, perform as many fast repetitions as possible. You can even cheat a little here. Don't worry if you can't get your elbows to ear level, just keep them moving. Within 15 to 20 seconds your deltoids should be totally exhausted. You will not be able to raise your elbows.

Super-slow set 1: Note the three selector pins in the weight stack.

Super-slow set 2: Have an assistant quickly remove the bottom selector pin.

Lateral raise: Lead with your elbows and move very slowly into the contracted position.

In fact, your training partner will probably have to pry you out of the machine.

Using the Super-Slow Routine

The super-slow breakdown routine severely stresses the deltoids. Such stress on the deltoids usually requires 72 hours for the overcompensation process to occur. Thus, it's a good idea to use this routine only twice in a week.

Give the super-slow breakdown routine a trial for at least two weeks and you can put your wool sweaters away forever.

Super-slow set 3: Continue the slow speed of movement until momentary muscular exhaustion.

Nautilus Shoulder Routine

Date					
Super-slow lateral raise, decrease by 20%					
Super-slow lateral raise, decrease by 20%					
Super-slow lateral raise					

CHAPTER 14
DOUBLE PRE-EXHAUSTION
FOR STRONG,
MUSCULAR THIGHS

A properly performed set on the Nautilus compound leg machine," Arthur Jones says, "should leave you feeling as if you had just climbed a tall building with your car tied to your back."

"The first time I tried the Nautilus compound leg machine," Mike Mentzer remembers, "I felt such pain and agony that I didn't want to look at it for a month, yet alone again in the same week. But the muscle-building results were so dramatic, I couldn't stay away for longer than 96 hours."

The Nautilus compound leg machine consists of two exercises: the leg extension and the leg press, which are performed in a pre-exhaustion fashion. When these exercises are done back to back, the quadriceps muscles of the frontal thighs are worked to a deep state of exhaustion. Once you've experienced the pre-exhaustion technique on the Nautilus compound leg machine, you suddenly realize what truly productive exercise is for the frontal thighs.

Now there's even a more productive way to strengthen your thighs. This method has been appropriately named double pre-exhaustion.

Double Pre-Exhaustion

Normal pre-exhaustion training is performed when a single-joint movement is immediately followed by a multiple-joint movement.

In the compound leg machine, for example, the leg extension is the single-joint movement and the leg press is the multiple-joint movement. The leg extension involves the muscles of the knee joint only. The leg press works the muscles surrounding the hip, knee, and ankle joints. The leg extension therefore pre-exhausts the quadriceps. Then before the frontal thighs can recover, the leg press brings into action the gluteals, hamstrings, and gastroc-soleus to force the quadriceps to a deeper state of exhaustion.

Double pre-exhaustion for the thighs goes a

Leg press: Try to establish a rhythm on this exercise.

Boyer Coe's muscular thighs. *(Photo by John Balik)*

step further. Instead of performing two exercises back to back, you perform three in a row. The three Nautilus exercises are as follows:

1. Leg press
2. Leg extension
3. Duo squat

Let's examine each exercise in detail.

Leg press: The leg press performed on the Nautilus compound leg machine primarily involves the quadriceps and hamstrings, and to a lesser degree, the gluteals and gastroc-soleus. When the leg press is performed first, the seat back should not be pulled forward to an extreme position. In fact, it is probably best to keep it in the same position you use in performing the leg extension. This allows more quadriceps and less gluteal involvement.

Place your feet in a slightly pigeon-toed fashion on the foot pedals. Smoothly straighten both legs. Do not slam into the lockout. Lower slowly until the weight touches the stack and repeat until momentary muscular exhaustion. Such exhaustion should occur between 8 and 12 repetitions. After the last repetition, slide your feet down, flip up the foot pedals, lean forward, and place your feet behind roller pads. Immediately start doing the leg extension.

Leg extension: Your quadriceps will be partially exhausted from the leg press. But you still should be able to do 8 to 12 repetitions of the leg extension with a fairly heavy resistance. Try to keep your head against the seat back, relax your face, and avoid excessive gripping of the handles. Be sure to pause for a second in the fully contracted position, but do not pause when the weights touch the stack. Even though your thighs will be screaming for mercy, grind out as many repetitions as possible. On the last repetition, someone should assist you in running to the duo squat machine. Granted, you won't feel like running, but do the best you can. To take full advantage of this super

Leg extension: Move quickly from the leg press to the extension.

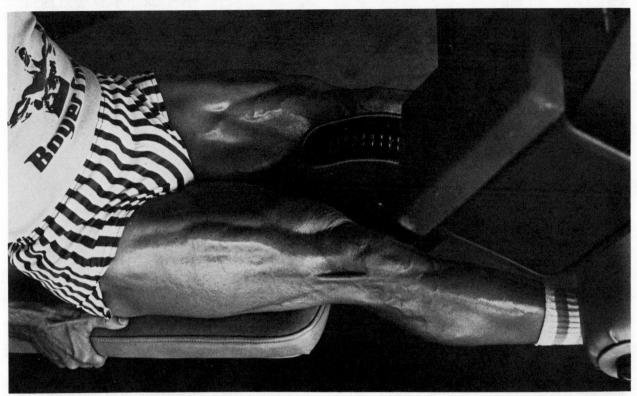

Pause briefly in the contracted position.

Duo squat: Straighten both legs and alternate back and forth between your right and left legs until failure.

pre-exhaustion routine, it is important to move from the second to the third exercise in *3 seconds*.

Duo squat: The resistance and the seat position on the duo squat machine should be adjusted beforehand. You should just barely be able to straighten both legs. The greater range of movement of the duo squat, as compared to the leg press, requires much more involvement of your gluteals. Thus, it takes the strength of your rested gluteals to force your burned-out quadriceps to keep contracting with each repetition. Try to perform at least 12 complete repetitions with each leg.

Other Double Pre-Exhaustion Routines for the Thighs

You can devise other routines for your thighs that involve double pre-exhaustion. Each series should be composed of three exercises, which are performed back to back with only minimum rest in between. Examples of such routines are as follows:

Hamstrings—Adductor Emphasis
1. Leg curl
2. Hip adduction
3. Duo squat
Hamstrings—Gluteal Emphasis
1. Leg curl
2. Duo hip and back
3. Duo squat
Hamstrings Emphasis
1. Leg curl
2. Hip adduction
3. Duo hip and back
Hamstrings Emphasis
1. Duo hip and back
2. Leg curl
3. Duo squat
Quadriceps Emphasis
1. Leg extension
2. Hip flexion
3. Duo squat

Less, Not More

If a properly performed set on the compound leg machine makes you feel as if you'd just climbed a tall building with your car tied to your back, then the double pre-exhaustion routine will double that feel!

Because of the unusual demands placed on your recovery ability, do not perform the double pre-exhaustion cycle for your legs more than twice a week. And even twice a week may be too demanding on your recovery ability for best results. If this is the case, then once a week will produce the best possible strengthening of your thighs.

"If in doubt, always do less exercise, not more," is Arthur Jones's constant advice to advanced bodybuilders. "The ones who listen get results. The ones who don't continue on the treadmill!"

Mike Mentzer's Thigh Routine

When Mike Mentzer performs double pre-exhaustion for his thighs, all other activity stops in the gym. The resistance he handles is so heavy that it causes the floor to vibrate.

Mike's July 18, 1983, leg routine was composed of the following:

1. Leg press		350/11
2. Leg extension		300/9
3. Duo squat		460/18

"Double pre-exhaustion," Mike says, "compared to normal pre-exhaustion, makes a much greater demand on my recovery ability. Because of the weight I can handle, my body only needs such a workout once every two weeks. But the muscle-building results are fantastic."

A double pre-exhaustion routine that works especially well for women bodybuilders is the one with hamstrings-gluteal emphasis. Shown here is the contracted position of the duo hip and back machine. *(Photo by Inge Cook)*

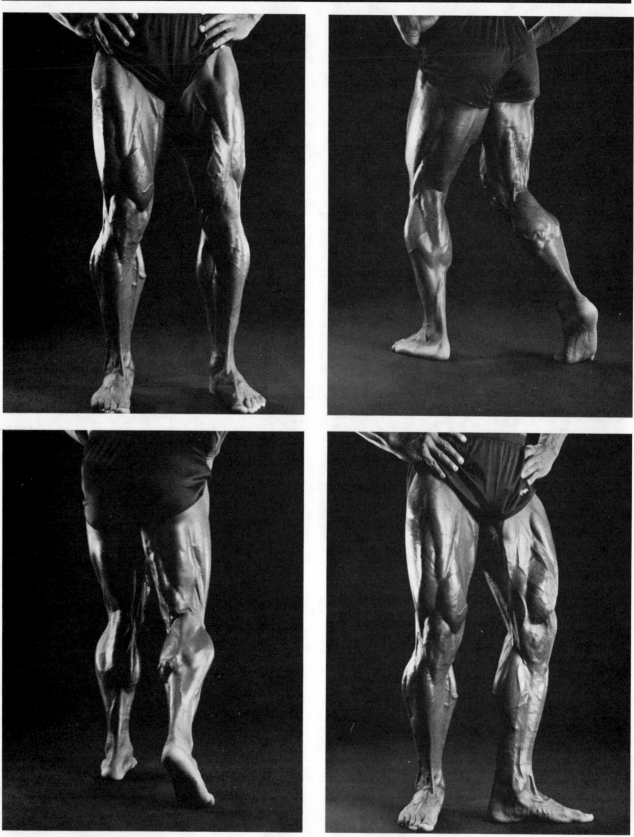

Boyer Coe's quadriceps and hamstrings look good from all angles. *(Photos by John Balik)*

Nautilus Thigh Routines

Primary Routine

Date					
Leg press					
Leg extension					
Duo squat					

Hamstrings—Adductor Emphasis

Date			
Leg curl			
Hip adduction			
Duo squat			

Hamstrings—Gluteal Emphasis

Date			
Leg curl			
Duo hip and back			
Duo squat			

Hamstrings Emphasis

Date			
Leg curl			
Hip adduction			
Duo hip and back			

Hamstrings Emphasis

Date			
Duo hip and back			
Leg curl			
Duo squat			

Quadriceps Emphasis

Date			
Leg extension			
Hip flexion			
Duo squat			

CHAPTER 15
A THREE-MINUTE THIGH PROGRAM

Have you reached a plateau or sticking point in training your thighs? Has your progress been at a standstill for several weeks? Are you using the same weights on the leg machines this month that you used last month?

If you answered yes to any or all of the above questions, then you may want to try this three-minute thigh routine.

Properly performed, the routine will quickly force your body out of its training rut. And it will definitely stimulate muscular size and strength increases in your thighs.

Let's look at this routine generally and then specifically.

Three Minutes or Bust

To perform this routine, you'll need access to the Nautilus duo squat machine. Three exercises are done back to back:

1. Akinetic squat performed with the movement-restraining bar in place, immediately followed by
2. Double-legged half squat, immediately followed by
3. One-legged alternating squat performed in the normal fashion

Akinetic squat: The movement-restraining bar must be in the center position to perform akinetic squats. The bar is also used in another style of squatting called infimetric. The primary difference between infimetric and akinetic is that with infimetric the selector pin is not used, while in akinetic a predetermined amount of resistance is selected.

To perform akinetic squats correctly, you'll need to use approximately four plates, or 100 pounds, *less* than you would normally handle on the one-legged alternating version.

With the seat adjusted properly, straighten both legs until contact is made with the movement-restraining stop. For one leg to straighten, the

Akinetic squat: Try to keep constant tension for a full 60 seconds. Make sure an assistant keeps time for you.

Remove the restraining bar from the middle position.

Ellington Darden keeps time as Boyer Coe performs akinetic squats.

Double-legged half squat: Go for another 60 seconds.

One-legged alternating squat: Use your buttocks to force your thighs to a deeper state of exhaustion.

other leg must bend. Slowly and smoothly straighten the right leg and bend the left. Then straighten the left and bend the right. If your legs are in perfect synchronization, the top of the weight stack will remain in contact with the movement-restraining stop. The weight stack will stay in the same position throughout the entire exercise. This is ideal. If the weight stack drops even slightly, you are making the exercise easier.

Akinetic squats are the hardest of the three squatting exercises. That's why they are performed first in the thigh cycle. Try to perform the repetitions smoothly and slowly for at least 45 seconds, but not more than 60 seconds.

This is no easy task. Within 6 or 7 repetitions you'll be feeling an intense burn in your thighs.

When you can no longer keep the top of the weight stack in contact with the movement-restraining stop, lower the resistance with both legs. Quickly have an assistant move the restraining bar to the side position. You're now ready to begin the second exercise in the cycle.

Double-legged half squat: Straighten both legs together. Your seat will be properly adjusted if the cam is fully unwound when your legs are straight. Lower the weight slowly with both legs until the weight stack touches and straighten your legs smoothly.

The first several repetitions of the double-legged half squat will be the hardest, so don't give up. Continue performing half squats for a full 60 seconds. If you have to rest toward the end of the set, do so by pausing for several seconds in the straight-legged position.

Ideally, you should strive to use the same resistance on the half squats as you used on the akinetic squats. If you are unable to continue for at least 45 seconds, however, your assistant should quickly reduce the weight by approximately 25 pounds.

You are now two-thirds of the way through your thigh cycle. For best results, you must immediately start performing the third exercise.

One-legged alternating squat: Both the akinetic and half squats have effectively pre-exhausted your quadriceps. With the one-legged alternating squats, your gluteal and hamstring muscles will now force your quadriceps to a deeper level of exhaustion. The reason your gluteals and hamstrings are involved more on the third exercise than the first and second is that the possible range of movement is greater around the hip joint.

Use the same weight and seat position for the one-legged alternating squats that you used for the half squats. Straighten both legs. Hold your left leg straight while your right slowly bends and comes back as far as possible. Push out smoothly with your right leg until it is straight. Hold your right leg straight and bend your left leg. Push out smoothly with your left leg. Alternate between your right and left legs for 60 seconds. Your assistant should call out your time in seconds as you near completion of this last exercise in the cycle.

Other Important Guidelines

One unique factor about this three-minute thigh cycle is that rather than counting repetitions, you count elapsed time. This is why it is important to have an assistant or training partner who has a watch with a second hand. You should try to fatigue your thigh muscles momentarily on each exercise somewhere between 45 and 60 seconds. If you cannot perform the exercise for 45 seconds, the resistance is too heavy. If you can do over 60 seconds of a movement, the weight is too light. Ideally, you should try to do the same amount of resistance on each of the three exercises.

To break your sticking point or plateau, use the three-minute thigh routine sparingly. It should be used twice a week for only two weeks. For example, you could perform it on Monday and Friday of the first week, and again on Monday and Friday of the second week. A basic workout, one which

does not involve the squat machine, would be used on Wednesday.

Perform the cycle at the beginning of your Monday and Friday workout. No other lower body exercises should be done. Limit your upper body training to six or seven additional Nautilus exercises. Thus, your entire workout on Monday and Friday would include one set of ten or fewer exercises.

After two weeks of such training, return to your normal workouts. You may repeat the three-minute thigh cycle once every three months.

If you're disappointed in the progress you've been making in training your legs, give the three-minute super thigh routine a trial. And don't be surprised if, the following week, your pants legs become significantly tighter.

Tom Platz displays his amazing thighs prior to one of his bodybuilding seminars.

Nautilus Three-Minute Thigh Routine

Date						
Akinetic squats						
Double-legged half squats						
One-legged alternating squats						

CHAPTER 16
THE DOUBLE-50 ROUTINE FOR BIGGER CALVES

Maybe it's because they're the focal point of the lower body? Maybe it's because they're easy to evaluate? Whatever the reason, calves can make or break a bodybuilder's physique.

Bill Grant has struggled for years trying to increase the size of his calf muscles. So have Roy Callendar, Robby Robinson, and Tony Pearson. They've probably tried multiple sets of every possible calf exercise, with the results being from poor to moderate depending on whom you're talking with.

On the other hand, Chris Dickerson, Mike Mentzer, and Tom Platz only work their calves on an infrequent basis. Yet their calves grow on almost any type of leg routine.

Why do some bodybuilders struggle while others triumph in the development of their calves?

The secret to large, shapely lower legs is extremely long gastrocnemius muscles. The longer the muscle bellies of the gastrocnemius are, the greater their size can be.

Every bodybuilder in the world who has large calves, with the much-desired low-diamond shape on the medial side of the lower leg, has long gastrocnemius muscles. Long gastrocnemius muscles are rare; perhaps as few as one in a million men have them.

The other extreme, short gastrocnemius muscles, is more common, especially among black bodybuilders. The typical black bodybuilder's gastrocnemius, when contracted, forms a thin knotted muscle high on the back calf.

Unfortunately, your muscles cannot be lengthened by training. Your muscle belly lengths are entirely based on genetics.

But don't give up. Regardless of the length of gastrocnemius muscles, you can increase their size. Just be realistic in your expectations.

Below is a tried-and-proved routine that's guaranteed to shock your calves into becoming larger

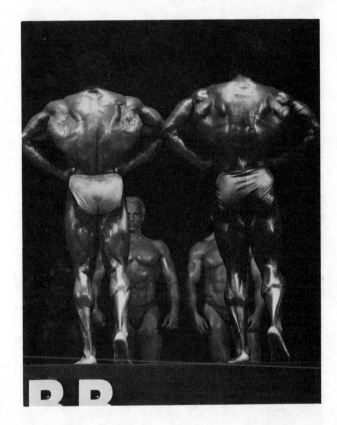

Tony Pearson (left) and Robby Robinson (right) have both inherited short gastrocnemius muscles.

The long gastrocnemius muscles are clearly visible in Tom Platz's calves.

Raise your heels smoothly, pause in the contracted position, lower slowly, and repeat for at least 25 repetitions.

Calf raise, set 1: Position the belt around your hips and stabilize your upper body with your hands.

After set 1, massage your calves for 60 seconds. Perform set 2 in a similar manner to set 1.

and stronger.

The Routine

The double-50 calf routine is what the name implies: two sets of 50 repetitions of the calf raise. But the sets, which are performed on the Nautilus multi-exercise machine, are done in an unusual manner.

Let's follow Boyer Coe through the double-50 routine.

Set 1: Boyer uses 50 pounds less on the multi-exercise machine than he would normally handle for 12 repetitions. Even so, he still uses the entire weight stack for his first set. With the belt in place, he places the balls of his feet on the first step. He adjusts the U-shaped dipping bars so they are level with his elbows.

In the normal calf raise Boyer lifts and lowers his heels while keeping his knees locked. The double-50 modifies the standard calf raise in two ways. First, there's a definite pause in the contracted, as well as the stretched, position. Second, when he can no longer do the positive part of the movement without cheating, he grasps the overhead parallel bars and pulls with his arms to get into the contracted position. Boyer usually gets 25 repetitions in strict form before he calls on his arms for assistance.

The last 10 repetitions are torture for Boyer. But he still manages to pause briefly in both the contracted and stretched positions.

After the final repetition, Boyer slips out of the belt, sits on the steps, and gently kneads his calves with his hands. Sixty seconds later, he's ready for set 2.

Set 2: The same weight is used by Boyer for set 2. And the style of performance is the same as it was for set 1. The only difference is that Boyer tires in the positive phase sooner, usually at about repetition 20. And naturally the pain comes sooner.

"Being able to work through the pain barrier,"

Continue by performing negative-emphasized repetitions. Grasp the overhead bars and pull with your upper body.

Boyer says, "is something advance bodybuilders must learn to cope with. Some bodybuilders deal with the pain by imagining something pleasant. But in my training, I've had success by focusing on the pain. Concentrating on the pain in my calves actually makes it seem less."

Boyer performs the last 30 repetitions with the help of his arms, in a negative-emphasized style. And he's careful not to just drop through the negative movement. His heels are always lowered slowly, as they must be for maximum growth stimulation.

Frequency

In all probability, the double-50 will make your calves extremely sore. The soreness, however, will not occur until 48 to 72 hours after the workout. You can combat some of the soreness by performing the routine three days in a row. After three consecutive-day workouts, your calves will need at least 48 hours of rest. Thereafter, best results will occur if you train your lower legs on three nonconsecutive days each week. For example, train them on Monday, Wednesday, and Friday, or on Tuesday, Thursday, and Saturday.

The double-50 routine is too demanding for year-round training. After two weeks of working your calves in the described fashion, you'd be advised to return to your regular calf routine. In four months or so, you might want to give it another trial for two weeks.

It is very easy to overwork your calves, or any other body part for that matter. High-intensity exercise is the key factor in muscular growth, but it also makes a severe demand on your body's recovery ability. If your body's recovery ability becomes depleted, then your muscles will not grow—regardless of the intensity of the exercise.

If this routine, performed as recommended, doesn't stimulate your calves to grow, you're probably overworking other muscles of your body. An entire high-intensity workout for all your major muscles should seldom last longer than 30 minutes. And such a workout should be performed only three times weekly.

Remember, that for the most efficient muscle-building results, your workouts must be high in intensity but brief in duration. And the calf muscles are not an exception.

Give the double-50 routine a try and break through your own pain barrier. You'll be rewarded with bigger calves.

Nautilus Double-50 Calf Routine

Date						
Calf raise with negative emphasis						
Calf raise with negative emphasis						

CHAPTER 17
ADD ½ INCH
TO YOUR ARMS
IN A WEEK

If you are dissatisfied with the size of your upper arms, why not try this special arm program? It's brief, efficient, and productive. In fact, this routine takes just five minutes to perform. That's right—five minutes! But during that five minutes your biceps and triceps will burn, pump, and ache like nothing you've ever experienced.

This new arm-building program—tested at the Nautilus Research Center in Lake Helen, Florida—has never failed to produce significant improvements in muscular size and strength.

If you progress in your workouts as directed and get adequate rest, you'll be rewarded with measurable increases in the circumference of your upper arms. Most bodybuilders can expect to add ½ inch of muscle mass to their upper arms in a week and a full inch after a month.

Your biceps and triceps are worked three times a week. On Mondays and Fridays, Arm Routine 1 is performed. On Wednesday, you do Arm Routine 2. Either routine is performed last in your overall workout.

Arm Routine 1

Routine 1 is executed on Monday and Friday of each week. You perform one set of four different exercises, two for the biceps and two for the triceps:

1. Multi-biceps curl (both arms together), immediately followed by
2. Chin, negative only
Rest for 30 seconds.
3. Multi-triceps extension (both arms together), immediately followed by
4. Dips, negative only

Multi-biceps curl: A resistance should be selected on the multi-biceps machine that allows you to perform between 8 and 12 strict repetitions. Pay particular attention to your speed of movement. Each repetition should be performed

Multi-biceps curl: Strive for full-range movements while keeping your elbows stable.

The award-winning peak of Boyer Coe's left biceps.

Chin, negative only: Lower your body slowly.

slowly and smoothly with no jerking or sudden movements.

When no further repetitions can be completed on the curls, you should immediately get out of the machine and run to the multi-exercise machine and start performing negative chin-ups. If more than 3 seconds elapse between these two exercises, the effect will be reduced.

Chin, negative only: For negative chin-ups, the multi-exercise machine must be preadjusted. The carriage must be at the correct height and the crossbar should be in the forward position. Quickly climb the stairs, place your chin over the crossbar, and bend your knees. Take 8 to 10 seconds to slowly, inch by inch, lower your body until your arms are completely straight. Immediately climb back to the top position and repeat the lowering movements for at least 8 slow repetitions. When 12 or more negative chin-ups are performed, you should attach additional resistance to your hips by using the belt, movement arm, and selectorized weight stack. After negative chins, you may rest for 30 seconds.

Multi-triceps extension: When seated properly in this machine, your shoulders should be slightly lower than your elbows. Smoothly straighten both arms by pushing the movement arms with the sides of your hands. Slowly lower the resistance and repeat for 8 to 12 repetitions.

When the final repetition is completed, run to the multi-exercise machine and do negative dips.

Dip, negative only: Climb into the top position with your arms locked, bend your knees, and lower slowly until your arms are fully bent. This lowering movement should take at least 8 seconds. Quickly step up to the starting position and continue for 8 to 12 repetitions. Additional resistance can be attached to the weight belt when you exceed 12 repetitions in strict form.

Multi-triceps extension: Concentrate on isolating your triceps.

Dip, negative only: Count to eight as your arms bend.

One-repetition chinup: Perform only one repetition as slowly as you can. Move instantly to the curl.

Multi-biceps curl: Curl the movement arms smoothly for at least 8 repetitions.

Infimetric curl: Place the movement-restraining bar in the middle and do 30 seconds of constant-tension curls.

Arm Routine 2

Routine 2 is performed on Wednesday of each week. It also consists of one set of four different exercises:

1. One repetition chin-up (30 to 60 seconds raising and 30 to 60 seconds lowering), immediately followed by
2. Multi-biceps curl (both arms together), instantly followed by infimetric curls on the same machine

Rest for 30 seconds.

3. One repetition dip (30 to 60 seconds raising and 30 to 60 seconds lowering), immediately followed by
4. Multi-triceps extension (both arms together), instantly followed by infimetric extensions on the same machine

One-repetition chin-up: The one-repetition chin-up is a demanding exercise. The objective is to make that single repetition as intense and slow as possible. From a hanging, underhand position with arms straight, take as long as possible to get your chin over the bar. Try to move a fraction of an inch and hold, another fraction of an inch and hold, and so on. Remain in each position briefly (without lowering) and move up inch by inch until your chin is above the bar. Have a friend who has a watch with a second hand call out the time in seconds (5, 10, 15, 20) to you as the exercise progresses. Once you've achieved the top position, lower yourself in exactly the same manner. Again, a friend or training partner should call out your time in seconds. Begin this movement with 30 seconds up and 30 seconds down. Add 5 seconds to both the positive and negative phases each workout. When you can perform 60 seconds up and 60 seconds down, use the weight belt to make the movement harder.

Multi-biceps curl: Doing curls immediately after the one-repetition chin-up will reduce your existing level of strength in the curl approximately 50 percent. In other words, you should use about half of the resistance that you would normally handle for 8 to 12 repetitions. Execute as many repetitions as possible with this reduced resistance on the multi-biceps machine.

After the final repetition, your training partner removes the selector pin from the weight stack and places the movement-restraining stop into the center position. Curl both arms until contact is made with the movement-restraining stop. In order for one arm to bend, the other arm must unbend or straighten. You can vary the force by resisting more or less with the unbending arm.

Begin the infimetric curls in a slow deliberate fashion for several repetitions. Gradually increase the force and the speed of movement. Continue for about 30 seconds or until you are not strong enough to keep the weight in contact with the rubber stop. Your biceps should be crying for mercy.

Have a quick drink of water, if you'd like, and get ready to work your triceps.

One-repetition dip: The one-repetition dip is performed in a similar fashion to the one-repetition chin-up. Start the dip in the bottom, stretched position. Take 30 to 60 seconds to move to the top and an equal amount of time to lower. Your training partner should make sure that he paces you properly by calling out your raising and lowering times in seconds.

Multi-triceps extension: Be certain the multi-triceps machine is preset before the dip is executed, because you have to run from one exercise to the next. The weight you've selected on the multi-triceps should allow you to perform from 8 to 12 repetitions.

When the last repetition is finished, the selector pin should be removed and the movement-restraining stop placed into the center position. Begin the infimetric triceps extension. As one arm straightens, the other arm bends. Right, left, right, left, right, left—smooth, forceful repetitions will

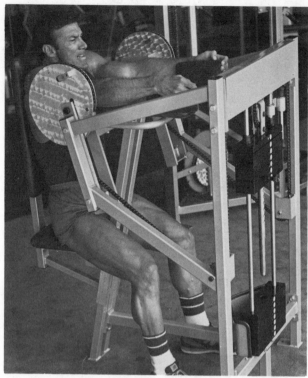

One-repetition dip: Make your triceps beg for mercy on this slow movement.

Multi-triceps extension: Use approximately 50 percent of the resistance that you would normally employ and do the repetitions in strict form.

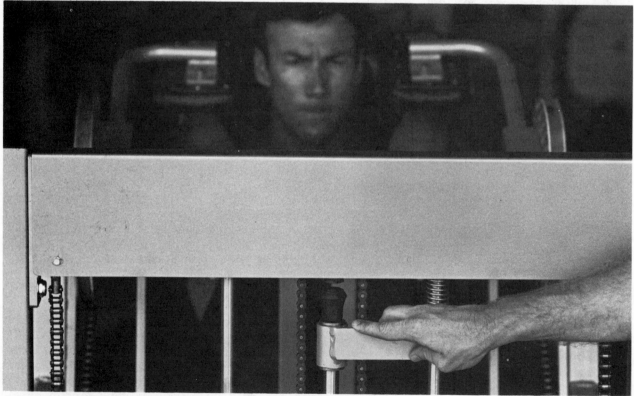

Infimetric extension: Move the bar quickly into the center position.

An interesting comparison of side arm poses by Samir Bannout and Bertil Fox.

Work one triceps against the other until total muscular exhaustion.

cause your triceps to burn and pump as never before. Continue for at least 30 seconds or until your arms can no longer straighten.

Maximizing Results

For maximum results, do only *one* set of each of the four exercises in Routine 1 on Monday and Friday. The same holds true for Routine 2, which is executed on Wednesdays.

Do not continue to work your arms in this manner for longer than one month. Such a program is too demanding. Your arms would soon become overtrained and your motivation would be diminished. After one month, return to your normal style of training. You may repeat the intense arm cycle once every four months.

High-intensity exercise is the stimulus for muscular growth. The higher the intensity, the briefer the exercise must be. If you feel you need more exercise for your upper arms, one of two things is occurring: You are either reducing the intensity of each exercise by stopping short of momentary muscular exhaustion, or you are failing to isolate the appropriate muscle group by cheating on each exercise.

Once your biceps and triceps have been stimulated to grow, they must be *permitted* to grow. They are permitted to grow *not* by performing more exercise, but by obtaining more rest. Recuperation is as important as high-intensity exercise.

Another important factor in building bigger upper arms is your ability to record accurately each of your workouts. Records are necessary in any progressive training. Include the date, time of day, order of exercises, resistance, repetitions, sets, and overall training time. This recording is often best accomplished immediately after each exercise by a training partner.

A reliable training partner can add consistency to your workouts. He tells you when to slow down, to hold your head back, to relax your lower body when working your arms. You must be reminded to eliminate excessive gripping and facial expressions, to do the last repetition, to hustle quickly from one machine to the next, and to perform numerous other fine points that make each Nautilus exercise harder and more productive.

The key to building bigger arms is hard, slow, strict, brief, supervised exercise followed by adequate rest. Try the recommended Nautilus program consistently for one month and watch your upper arms grow!

Nautilus Arm Routines

ARM ROUTINE 1

Date					
Multi-biceps curl					
Chin, negative only					
Multi-triceps extension					
Dip, negative only					

ARM ROUTINE 2

Date					
One repetition, slow chin-up					
Multi-biceps curl					
Infimetric curl					
One repetition, slow dip					
Multi-triceps extension					
Infimetric extension					

CHAPTER 18
MORE ON
MASSIVE ARMS

"**I**n the summer of 1970, I trained Sergio Oliva for the Mr. Universe contest," Arthur Jones recalls. "One night I was looking through some old *Strength & Health* magazines and I came across a close-up of John McWilliams's arm. McWilliams had entered several national physique contests in the latter 1940s.

"The caption under the picture said that it was a grossly distorted photograph taken with a wide-angle lens of a claimed 21-inch arm. I found out later, in fact, that *Strength & Health* had refused to publish the photograph for several years because they thought it was faked.

"In truth, McWilliams's arm was distorted, but the photograph was not. His arm was unbelievably large and muscular and measured at least 21 inches in his best condition.

"Well, the next day, I showed Sergio the picture of McWilliams's arm. Sergio, who had a cold 20¼-inch arm at that time, studied the photo, looked up at me, shook his head, and said, 'Arthur, that's too big!'"

Jones's story about Sergio always draws laughs from the bodybuilders who are listening. Every one of them would like to have arms that are "too big."

And Ray Mentzer is no exception.

Ray, at a height of 5 feet 11 inches, weighed 260 pounds when he trained in Florida during the spring of 1983. His upper arm was 20⅛ inches.

"This is the largest arm I've measured since Sergio's 20¼," said Jones. "Ray, I think you've got the potential to have the largest arm in the history of bodybuilding."

"Let's do it," Ray said as he smiled as only a man with 20-inch arms can smile.

Here's one of the routines that Ray Mentzer followed in his quest for 21-inch arms.

Biceps Cycle

Ray uses three exercises in his biceps cycle:

Another view of the massive arm of Ray Mentzer, which measured 20⅜ inches when this picture was taken. *(Photo by Ellington Darden)*

The curl on the Nautilus multi-biceps machine is one of Boyer Coe's favorite exercises.

Sergio Oliva's flexed upper arms are actually wider than his head is high—the distance from the bottom of his triceps to the top of his biceps exceeds the distance from below his chin to above the top of his head. (Photo by Inge Cook)

Bev Francis and Carla Dunlap compare arms at the 1983 World Cup Bodybuilding Championships in Las Vegas. Bev, because of her unusual muscular size and strength, created a lot of controversy at this contest.

1. Multi-biceps cheating curl, immediately followed by

2. Multi-biceps regular curl, immediately followed by

3. Behind-neck pulldown

Multi-biceps cheating curl: Ray loads the multi-biceps machine with approximately 40 percent more resistance than he handles in the normal fashion. To get a heavy enough resistance, he must pin several 25-pound plates on the weight stack.

In a standing position, Ray cheats the movement arms to the contracted position. He sits down and lowers the movement arms to a slow count of 8. Then he quickly stands and cheats the movement arms back to the contracted position and repeats the lowering very slowly.

The first several repetitions will feel easy. Don't be fooled. They soon get very hard. By the 7th or 8th repetition your biceps will feel as if they're being contracted and stretched as never before. In fact, they are.

Ray tries to get between 8 and 12 repetitions on the cheating curl. Regardless of the repetitions, he continues until his biceps can no longer control the downward movement of the weight. Instantly, without resting, the weight on the machine is lowered by approximately 50 percent for regular curls.

Multi-biceps curl: Regular curls, both arms together, are performed in strict style for 8 to 12 repetitions. Ray pauses in the contracted position of each repetition and intensely squeezes his biceps.

Again, the initial repetitions will seem almost too easy. By repetition 7, however, your biceps will be on fire. Be determined to do another 3 or 4 repetitions if at all possible. Don't cheat. Keep the form strict.

Ray moves quickly from the multi-biceps machine to the torso-arm machine and belts in for the behind-neck pulldown.

Multi-biceps cheating curl: Stand up, grasp the handles, and cheat-curl the movement arms into the contracted position. Sit down and slowly lower.

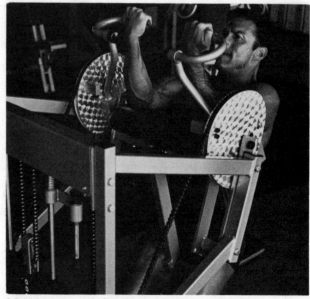

Multi-biceps curl: Grind out at least 8 repetitions in strict form.

Behind-neck pulldown: Use your lats to force your biceps to work even harder.

Behind-neck pulldown: The behind-neck pull-down brings into action Ray's rested latissimus dorsi muscles to force his biceps to a deeper level of exhaustion. With a parallel grip, Ray leans forward and pulls the bar behind his neck. He pauses briefly in the contracted position and lowers the weight slowly to the starting position, then repeats for 8 to 12 repetitions.

After a big drink of water, Ray is ready to move to the triceps cycle.

Triceps Cycle

The triceps are worked on the multi-exercise machine and the double chest machine.

1. Triceps extension with towel on multi-exercise, immediately followed by
2. Triceps extension with towel on multi-exercise with 20 percent less resistance, immediately followed by
3. Decline press

Triceps extension with towel: Ray loops a lightweight towel through the waist belt, which is connected to the movement arm. He grasps one end of the towel in each hand, stands, and faces away from the machine. His elbows are near his ears, and his arms are bent. The towel can be adjusted if necessary to keep the weight stack separated.

Smoothly, Ray straightens his arms in a controlled fashion, being careful not to move his elbows. He pauses in the contracted position and lowers his hands slowly for a full stretch of his triceps. Ray performs as many repetitions as possible, but tries to keep them in the 8 to 12 range.

When he fails on the last repetition, he bends his knees so the weight stack will touch and an assistant immediately reduces the weight by approximately 20 percent. Ray stands and begins another set of triceps extensions.

Triceps extension with towel: The weight is 20 percent lighter, but the repetitions are harder in this set than the first. Ray resists cheating by con-

Triceps extension with towel: Keep your elbows high and stable. Your hands and forearms should be your only moving body part.

Reduce the resistance by 20 percent and begin the second set.

Perform as many slow, smooth extensions as possible.

Decline press: Keep your elbows low on this pressing movement and you'll feel it more in your triceps.

centrating on bringing into action the deeper fibers of his triceps as he methodically straightens his arms for another 8 to 12 repetitions.

"Nothing pumps my triceps as much as this exercise," Ray says as he drops the towel and runs to the double chest machine for the decline press.

Decline press: With the triceps almost completely fatigued, Ray now uses the strength of his pectorals and deltoids to push his triceps to their absolute limit. To accentuate his triceps even more, Ray keeps his elbows low by his sides during both the positive and negative movements. Again, he grinds out another 8 to 12 repetitions. When he can't quite straighten his arms, he'll often use his feet to help get three more forced repetitions.

Ray Mentzer's Challenge

"Three sets for the biceps and three sets for the triceps—repeated twice a week. That's my arm program for 21-inch guns," Ray Mentzer repeats. "And if I don't reach my goal from this routine soon enough, I'll do fewer sets, not more.

"Why don't you accept the Nautilus challenge and get massive arms now?"

Ray Mentzer's Arm Workout

The weight and repetitions that Ray Mentzer used July 7, 1983, on his biceps and triceps cycle are as follows:

Biceps Cycle

1. Multi-biceps cheating curl	225/9
2. Multi-biceps regular curl	110/10
3. Behind-neck pulldown	180/9

Triceps Cycle

1. Triceps extension with towel	130/10
2. Triceps extension with towel	100/8
3. Decline press	250/10

Nautilus Biceps and Triceps Cycles

BICEPS CYCLE

Date					
Multi-biceps cheating curl					
Multi-biceps regular curl					
Behind-neck pulldown					

TRICEPS CYCLE

Date					
Triceps extension with towel, decrease by 20%					
Triceps extension with towel					
Decline press					

CHAPTER 19
ARM AND SHOULDER TRAINING FOR WOMEN BODYBUILDERS

Puny and bony! That's the way I'd describe the arms and shoulders of most women bodybuilders," says Julie McNew.

Julie, a popular bodybuilder originally from Indiana, was training with Mike Mentzer in Florida during the summer of 1983.

"Well-developed arms and shoulders," Julie continues, "are just as important for women bodybuilders as they are for men. Yet, most women competitors seem to be afraid to train their upper body in a heavy, intense fashion. Women who want to enter bodybuilding competition should emphasize the training of their arms and shoulders. Doing so will definitely improve their overall symmetry."

Julie is right. Most women bodybuilders would have better overall symmetry if they had larger arms and shoulders.

In general, women have wider hips than men because of their hormones and genetic makeup. As compared to men, women also have narrower shoulders. The width and narrowness of these two focal points in the human body help to create an illusion. A woman bodybuilder, for example, who has wide hips and narrow shoulders appears to have wider hips than she actually does because of the narrowness of her shoulders.

Thus, any woman bodybuilder who wants her hips to appear narrower should broaden her shoulders. Broad, muscular shoulders nicely balance the female tendency to wide hips.

Besides broader shoulders, well-developed upper arms and forearms also make a woman's hips and thighs seem slimmer. This results in a more pleasing appearance when a woman is standing. Furthermore, larger arms allow a competitive bodybuilder more variety in her posing.

One of the keys to complete arm and shoulder development is muscle isolation, isolation of the biceps, triceps, and deltoids. Nothing isolates those muscles as well as Nautilus machines.

Julie McNew displays her arms and shoulders.

Julie McNew in the Nautilus compound position biceps machine.

"For the last three months," Julie says, "Mike Mentzer has been training me on Nautilus equipment, and I can see the impact it's making on my body. My arms and shoulders are stronger and more shapely than they've ever been."

The pictures of Julie McNew in this chapter clearly show that her biceps, triceps, deltoids, and forearm flexors and extensors could win the "Best Arms" award in any major women's bodybuilding competition.

Let's examine Julie's shoulder and arm routine.

Julie McNew's Routine

Julie does two exercises for her deltoids, two for her biceps, and two for her triceps. They are performed in this order:

1. Lateral raise, immediately followed by
2. Overhead press
3. Compound position biceps, immediately followed by
4. Supination on Sportsmate
5. Triceps pressdown on torso arm, immediately followed by
6. Pushup on floor

Lateral raise: The lateral raise isolates the middle deltoid and is best performed on the new Nautilus lateral raise machine. The primary movement of the double shoulder machine may be used if the new machine is not available.

Julie adjusts the seat so her shoulders are in line with the rotational axes of the cams. She grasps the handles and moves her elbows back until they are slightly behind her torso. Smoothly she raises her arms until her elbows are parallel with her ears. This raising movement takes two seconds. After a brief pause in the contracted position, she lowers slowly to the count of four. Julie continues performing repetitions until she cannot reach ear level with her elbows. Usually she fails between 10 and 12 repetitions. Immediately she moves to the overhead press.

Lateral raise: Keep the elbows back to involve more of the middle deltoids.

Overhead press: Extend your arms smoothly while keeping your elbows wide.

Compound position biceps, right arm: Concentrate on your biceps as you slowly bend your arm.

Compound position biceps, left arm: Switch sides and do as many repetitions as possible with your left arm.

Overhead press: The new overhead press should be used if it is available. If not, use the secondary portion of the double shoulder machine.

Julie places the seat into the highest position. She quickly fastens the seat belt and starts the pressing movement. The overhead press brings into action Julie's triceps to force her pre-exhausted deltoids to a deeper state of fatigue. Julie grinds out 8 to 12 repetitions, being careful not to arch her back during the last movements.

Compound position biceps: The biceps muscle has three functions: (1) to supinate the hand, (2) to flex the elbow, and (3) to raise the upper arm forward. For the biceps to contract fully, the hand must be supinated, the elbow must be bent, and the upper arm must be raised to ear level. The compound position biceps, more than any other Nautilus arm machine, provides the most complete contraction of the biceps.

Julie works her right biceps first. She adjusts the seat so her elbow is in line with the axis of the cam. She grasps the handle lightly and curls it to her shoulder. In this position, she pauses and contracts her biceps as intensely as possible. The weight is lowered slowly, and the curling and contraction are repeated for 8 to 12 repetitions. Julie then works the left biceps in the same manner by moving to the opposite side of the machine. The next exercise for Julie is supination on the Sportsmate.

Supination on Sportsmate: For several years, Nautilus manufactured a plastic rotary exercise device called Sportsmate. It is no longer being sold. If you can get access to one, do so. It provides direct, full-range exercise for the supination function of the biceps.

Julie holds the Sportsmate so her palms face each other. She places the unit on a wall with her forearms parallel to the floor. It is important that her elbows remain against her sides during the movement. Julie rotates her right hand and forearm as far clockwise as possible. At the same time, she resists the clockwise motion with her left arm. Then she twists with her left arm and resists with her right arm. In other words, the negative strength of one arm provides the positive resistance for the other arm. Julie alternately twists and resists for 8 to 12 repetitions of each arm.

"Working on the Sportsmate immediately after the compound position curls," Julie says, "really puts a peak on my biceps. It also puts me in a mood to work my triceps."

Triceps pressdown on torso arm: For this exercise, Julie loops a towel over the pulldown bar of the torso arm machine. She stands under the movement arm, grasps each end of the towel, and moves her elbows to a stable position by her sides. The weight is lifted slightly and both hands are in front of her chest. This is the starting position of the exercise.

Smoothly, without moving her elbows, Julie presses downward on the towel. As her elbows straighten, her hands are about 6 inches away from her hips. Keeping the hands away from the hips when the elbows are straight involves more of the triceps. Julie completes 10 strict repetitions of triceps pressdowns and immediately lies on the floor for a set of pushups.

Pushup: "But pushups are too easy," Julie said before she tried them immediately after triceps pressdowns. "By the 4th rep, however, I felt as if I'd performed at least 30 regular pushups."

The key to this unique effect is to release the towel on the torso arm and get on the floor in the pushup position in less than two seconds. With your hands under your shoulders and your body rigid, immediately start doing pushups. Smoothly push up by straightening your arms and slowly lower your body back to the floor. Lightly touch your chest and begin another repetition. Do as many repetitions as you can without cheating.

Supination on Sportsmate: Twist with your left biceps and resist with your right. Then twist with your right and resist with your left.

Triceps pressdown on torso arm: Push downward on the towel while keeping your elbows at your sides.

Pushup: Do the movements as strictly as possible and your triceps will feel like exploding.

"Even after four weeks of doing this triceps routine, I could only get 15 pushups. But wow! The effect on my arms is simply amazing. My triceps feel like inflated balloons for at least 30 minutes afterward."

Additional Comments

"I work my shoulders and arms twice a week," Julie says, "and I always work them last in my regular routine. To begin my regular routine, I usually do four exercises for my lower body: leg extension, hip adduction, hip abduction, and leg curl. Once a week, I'll use the duo squat machine and calf raise.

"After my legs are worked, I'll do one set for my lats, one set for my pecs, and one set for either my traps or lower back. Then I'll go into my shoulder and arm program.

"Oh yeah, one last thing: Once a week, usually on Friday at the end of my workout, I'll do a set of regular-grip chin-ups. Chin-ups are a great way to finish off my arms.

"Try this routine for a month," Julie says as she flexes her arms and smiles, "and I'll bet that your arms and shoulders will cease being puny and bony."

A double-biceps pose by Julie McNew. (Photo by Ellington Darden)

Nautilus Arm and Shoulder Routine for Women

Date						
Lateral raise						
Overhead press						
Compound position biceps						
Supination on Sportsmate						
Triceps pressdown on torso arm						
Pushup						

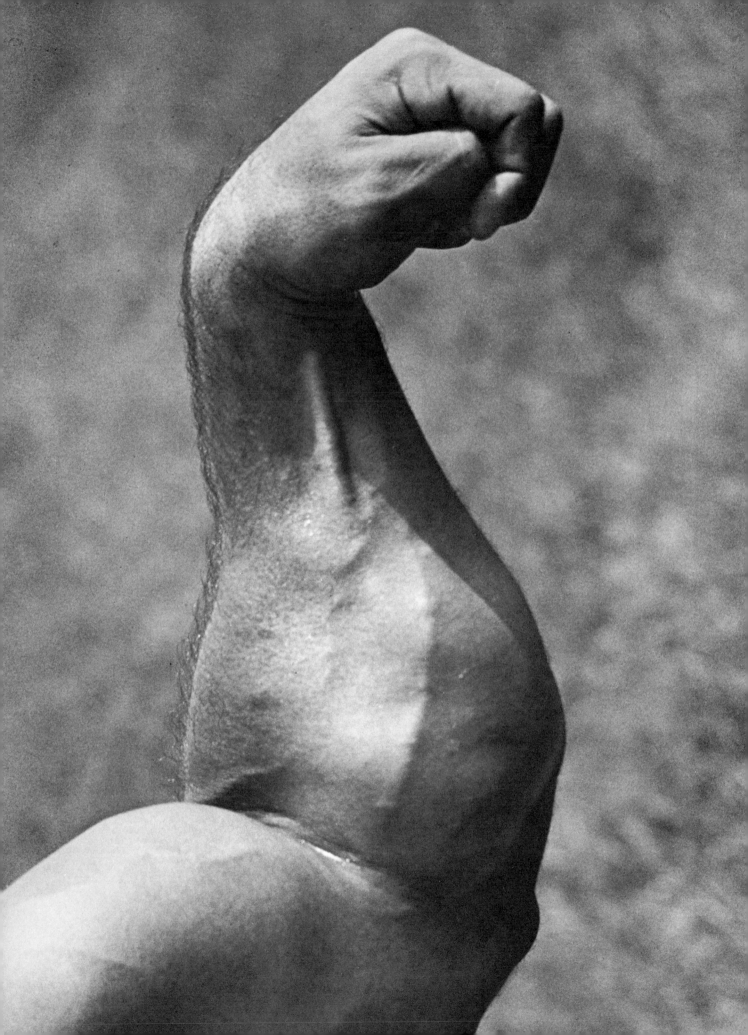

CHAPTER 20
FANTASTIC FOREARMS

Arthur Jones has always been interested in measurements, especially large muscular measurements.

"Bill Pearl's largest forearm measured 13¾ inches," Jones remembered. "Arnold Schwarzenegger's forearm was almost 14 inches and Franco Columbo's was 13¼ inches."

Jones was in a talkative mood. He had just finished training Boyer Coe in front of a small crowd of interested spectators at the Nautilus Television Studios in Lake Helen, Florida.

"The largest forearm I've ever measured," Jones continued, "was that of Sergio Oliva. Sergio's flexed forearms were a bit over 15½ inches.

"Casey Viator, however, had the largest difference between his wrist and forearm that I've ever measured. Casey had a 7½-inch wrist and almost a 15½-inch forearm. His forearm was over twice the size of his wrist.

"The key to Sergio's and Casey's fantastic forearms was their long muscle bellies. Their forearm flexor muscles extended almost to their wrist."

Among the crowd listening to Jones's description of forearm size were Mike and Ray Mentzer.

"Arthur, measure my wrist and forearm," Mike said as he moved out of the crowd.

"Okay," Arthur said as he carefully placed the tape around Mike's wrist. "Your right wrist measures 7½ inches. Now, keep your elbow straight, make a fist, flex your wrist, and contract your forearm."

The muscles in Mike's forearm contracted in bold relief. It looked at least 15 inches.

"It's 15¼ inches," Arthur said as he looked closely at the tape through his glasses.

"Measure mine," Ray said as he stepped forward and rolled up his right sleeve.

"Your right wrist is 7½ inches, the same as Casey's and the same as Mike's. Flex your forearm as hard as possible," challenged Arthur.

Ray's massive forearm looked as if he had a

The 15⁹⁄₁₆-inch cold forearm of Ray Mentzer. *(Photo by Lewis Green)*

Ray Mentzer's massive forearm. *(Photo by Ellington Darden)*

cluster of grapes the size of a football between his elbow and wrist.

"This is incredible. It's exactly 15⁹⁄₁₆ inches," Jones announced as the crowd moved closer for a better look. "Your forearm is approximately the same size as Sergio's, but your wrist is smaller. Ray, you probably have the largest, muscular forearm in the world today."

"Wait a second," said someone with a deep voice from the back of the room. "Measure my forearm."

The crowd laughed loudly as a small, skinny guy stood up and flexed his forearm, a forearm that measured no more than 10 inches.

"Your forearms can be improved through proper training," Jones said in a serious tone. "But under no conditions would they ever look like Ray's.

"At a glance, I can tell that your forearms have short muscle bellies and long tendon attachments. Ray has just the opposite: long muscle bellies and short tendon attachments.

"Maybe someone in the future will have bigger forearms than Ray. But if so, his daddy will be a gorilla."

Primary Forearm Exercises

The forearms are composed of many small and medium-size muscles. These muscles flex and extend the wrist, flex and extend the fingers, and supinate and pronate the hands. For full development of the forearms, you must provide progressive resistance for those six forearm functions. The following exercises can provide this required resistance.

1. Wrist curl on multi-exercise
2. Finger curl on multi-exercise
3. Reverse wrist curl on multi-exercise
4. Supination on Sportsmate
5. Pronation on Sportsmate
6. Finger extension in thick clay

Wrist curl on multi-exercise: Make sure your elbows are higher than your hands. If necessary, sit on several pads.

Curl the handles by flexing your wrists.

Finger curl on multi-exercise: Extend and flex your fingers for 8 to 12 repetitions.

Reverse wrist curl on multi-exercise: Grasp the handles tightly. Keep your forearms stable and do not lean back.

Reverse-curl the handles to the top position. Lower slowly and repeat.

Supination on Sportsmate: Emphasize the twisting action of the hands and forearms.

Pronation on Sportsmate: Concentrate on pushing, rather than twisting, with the hands and forearms. Be careful not to move your elbows.

Wrist curl on multi-exercise: In a seated position in front of the multi-exercise machine, attach the handle directly to the movement arm. Rest your forearms on your thighs and lean forward until the angle between your upper arm and forearm is less than 90 degrees. Grasp the bar firmly in the hands with a palms-up grip. Curl the handle smoothly to the contracted position. Pause, lower slowly, and repeat for 8 to 12 repetitions. Do not allow your forearms or torso to move. Do not extend the fingers. Keep the handle in the palms of your hands.

Finger curl on multi-exercise: Assume the same position as the wrist curl. Instead of moving your hands and flexing your wrists, simply extend the fingers. Curl the handle back to the hands and repeat for 8 to 12 repetitions.

Reverse wrist curl on multi-exercise: Assume the same position as the wrist curl except reverse your grip. Move your hands smoothly upward. Pause. Lower slowly to the starting position and repeat for 8 to 12 repetitions.

Supination on Sportsmate: Grasp the handles of the Sportsmate so your palms face each other. Hold the unit on the wall with your forearms parallel to the floor. Keep your elbows at your sides and do not lift them away during the movement. Rotate your right hand and forearm as far clockwise as possible. At the same time, resist the clockwise motion with your left arm. Reverse the procedure for your left arm. Repeat for 8 to 12 repetitions for each arm.

Pronation on Sportsmate: Assume the same position for pronation as you did for supination. To pronate, push with the hands and arms instead of twisting. Push and resist with each hand in an alternate fashion for 8 to 12 repetitions.

Finger extension in thick clay: Shove your clenched fists into a deep bucket of thick clay. The clay should be free of sand and mixed with water to a creamy consistency. Unclench and fully extend your fingers against the resistance provided from all directions by the clay. Do this rapidly and repeat it until your hands feel as if they are ready to drop off.

Forearm Tips

Your forearms should be worked toward the end of your routine immediately after your upper arms. For fastest results, you must work your forearms to the point of absolute failure. But equally important, this state of exhaustion must be reached within a short time.

It would be a mistake to include more than three of the six previously described forearm exercises in any one workout. Doing more than you need, or more than your muscles can take, can only hinder your progress.

You might do the wrist curl, finger curl, and reverse wrist curl during your first weekly workout. And at the next workout, perform supination, pronation, and the finger extension in clay.

Train your forearms intensely for six weeks and you'll be pleasantly surprised with their improvement. And if you're blessed with long muscle bellies in your forearms, see if you can build your flexed forearm to measure over twice the size of your wrist. If so, you'll be placed in an elite category that includes Sergio Oliva, Casey Viator, Mike Mentzer, and Ray Mentzer.

Nautilus Forearm Exercises

Date						
Wrist curl						
Finger curl						
Reverse wrist curl						
Supination on Sportsmate						
Pronation on Sportsmate						
Finger extension in clay						

CHAPTER 21
ATTACKING THE WAIST FROM ALL ANGLES

High-repetition sit-ups, side bends, leg raises, and twisting movements have been advocated for years as a way to remove fat from the waistline. The idea is that exercising the muscles of the midsection somehow burns the fat cells which overlie the muscles. Unfortunately, this is *not* the case.

The fat that is stored around your waistline is in a form called lipids. To be used as energy, the lipids must be converted to fatty acids. This is a very complex chemical procedure. To be used as fuel, the lipids must travel through the bloodstream to the liver. In the liver they must be converted to fatty acids, which are then transported to the working muscles.

This is well and good. But a problem arises because there are no direct pathways from the fat cells to the muscle cells. When fat is used for energy, it is mobilized primarily through the liver out of the multiple fat cells all over the body. The selection process that your body uses for mobilizing its fat stores is programmed by your genes. The mobilization process, in fact, is in the reverse order to which you store fat.

A typical bodybuilder, for example, might deposit fat first on the sides of his waist. Second, it might go over the navel area, then the hips, then the back, and finally the thighs. When he starts losing fat, it comes first from his thighs, then back, hips, navel area, and finally the sides of the waist.

Each person would have a slightly different ordering of favorite fat-storage spots. But there is most definitely an ordering. And that ordering is genetically determined and is not subject to change.

Spot reduction, therefore, is impossible. And anyone who recommends specific exercises for spot reducing is misinformed.

What matters most in losing fat is your overall consumption of calories. Your energy output must exceed your energy input. You must eat fewer

Tom Platz reveals his abdominals.

The amazing midsection of Johnny Fuller.

Rotary torso: Push with your right palm for right-to-left torso rotation.

Pause briefly in the contracted position and rotate slowly back to the starting position. Repeat.

Change sides and reverse the procedure for left-to-right rotation.

Abdominal: Make sure the axis of rotation of the machine is on the same level as your navel. Adjust the seat if necessary.

Move your torso forward and down by contracting your abdominals.

calories than you expend on a daily basis.

Spot *production* of the muscles of the waistline, however, is possible. You can selectively strengthen and develop your midsection muscles. Doing so will make your waist look and feel firmer.

Brief, infrequent, high-intensity exercise, combined with a reduced-calorie diet, is the best way to muscularize your waistline.

Waistline Machines

Your waistline is composed of many muscle groups. The most important are the rectus abdominis and iliopsoas on the front, the external and internal obliques on the sides, and the erector spinae on the back. Nautilus makes equipment that works each of these muscles.

1. Rotary torso machine: external and internal obliques
2. Abdominal machine: rectus abdominis
3. Lower back machine: erector spinae
4. Hip flexion machine: iliopsoas

Let's examine the proper way to use each of these machines.

Rotary torso: Straddle the seat on the right side of the machine and cross your ankles securely. Turn to the right and place your forearms on the sides of the pads. Your right palm should be firmly against the middle bar of the movement arm. Rotate your torso from right to left by pushing with your right palm. Do not use your triceps or biceps to push or pull the movement arm. Pause in the contracted position. Return slowly to the starting position and repeat for 8 to 12 repetitions. Straddle the seat on the left side of the machine and reverse the procedure for left-to-right torso rotation.

Abdominal (new machine): The new abdominal machine, unlike the older machine, eliminates the use of the arms in spinal flexion. Sit in the machine with the swivel pads in front of your chest. Adjust the seat until the axis of rotation is approximately parallel to your navel. Hook both feet under the bottom roller pads. Adjust the swivel pads on your chest to a comfortable position. Place your hands across your waist. Rotate your torso smoothly toward your thighs. Keeping your knees wide will place more stress on the rectus abdominis and less on the iliopsoas. Pause in the contracted position. Return slowly to the starting position and repeat for 8 to 12 repetitions.

Lower back: Enter the machine from the side by straddling the seat. Make sure you are seated on the seat bottom, not the angle between the seat bottom and the seat back. Your back should be underneath the highest roller pad. Stabilize your lower body by moving your thighs under the bottom roller pads. Place your feet firmly on the platform. Fasten the seat belt around your hips. Interlace your fingers across your waist. Move your torso backward smoothly until it is in line with your thighs. Pause in the contracted position. Return slowly to the starting position and repeat for 8 to 12 repetitions.

Hip flexion: Sit in the machine. Fasten the seat belt across your thighs. Lie back in a reclining position. Grasp the handles behind your head. Keep your torso and head on the seat back. Flex your hips smoothly by drawing your knees to your chest. Pause. Lower slowly to the starting position and repeat for 8 to 12 repetitions.

General Guidelines

• Don't make the mistake of training your midsection muscles more frequently or with higher repetitions than your other muscles. Remember, spot reduction is not possible.

• Perform only one set of each of the four exercises for 8 to 12 repetitions with as much weight as possible in good form.

• Train your midsection no more than three times a week.

• Attack your waistline from all angles, but keep the exercise brief.

Lower back: Stabilize your hips and thighs with the belt and thigh pads.

Extend your torso backward until it is in line with your thighs. Pause, lower slowly, and repeat.

Hip flexion: Keep your knees slightly apart as you begin
this movement.

Pause in the contracted position and try to lift your
buttocks. Lower slowly and repeat.

Nautilus Waist Exercises

Date						
Rotary torso						
Abdominal						
Lower back						
Hip flexion						

CHAPTER 22
EMPHASIZING THE NECK

The most massive neck I've ever seen," recalled Vic Tanny, Sr., "belonged to Frank Jares. Frank trained at my gym in California in the 1940s. He stood 5 feet 9½ inches, weighed about 225 pounds, and wrestled professionally under the name of Brother Frank. In his prime, Frank's neck measured at least 21 inches.

"Frank had an open challenge to anyone in my gym: 'Strangle me with your bare hands if you can,' he'd say each time he trained.

"Many big guys took him up on his challenge. Frank would flex his neck like a giant cobra. It was almost impossible, unless you had very large hands, to encircle his neck. No one even came close to strangling him. What a powerful neck he had."

"Vic, did you ever see Milo Steinborn in his heyday?" asked an interested bodybuilder. "His neck was supposed to be over 20 inches."

"I always admired Milo in my younger days," Tanny replied, "but I never had the chance to meet and talk with him."

Several weeks later, Vic did meet and talk with Steinborn. Milo, one of the last of the old-time strongmen, is 90 years of age and lives in Orlando. He still holds the world's record for squatting with over 500 pounds—unassisted, without the use of racks. To accomplish such a feat, Milo would stand the heavy barbell on end, squat to one side of it, lean into it and roll it across his shoulders, maintain his balance, and stand up from the low-squat position. He'd then perform several full squats and finally stop in the low position. Then he'd lean to the right and get out from under the barbell the same way he got into it—all unassisted! Try that sometime if you get bored with your workouts.

"When I walked into Milo's home," Tanny said, "I was surrounded by memories from the strongman era. On the front porch there were a half-dozen globe-type, shot-loading barbells and numerous odd-shaped kettlebells and molded dumbbells.

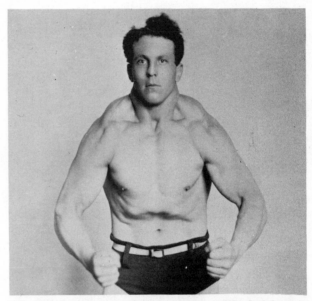

Milo Steinborn in 1921. *(Photo courtesy of Milo Steinborn.)*

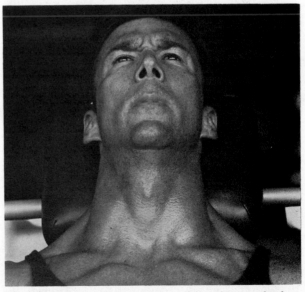

4-way neck, back extension: Lower the resistance slowly with your neck.

Boyer Coe on the Nautilus 4-way neck machine.

In the living room, one wall was filled with formal pictures of Milo and his family from Germany. Milo's study, located in the back of the house, was covered floor to ceiling with old photographs. More strongman pictures and many oversized posters were hanging in the garage, where Milo kept his wrestling mat.

"For over three hours we talked about the old days, the places he'd been, the athletes he'd wrestled, the weights he'd lifted, and the ways he'd trained. But you know, the thing that impressed me most about Milo was his neck. Even today at 90, it must measure a full 18 inches.

"In every one of the old photos of Milo that lined his walls, my eyes were drawn immediately to his neck. What thickness he had in his sternomastoids and trapezius muscles. Milo's neck in his prime was every bit as massive as Frank Jares's."

What was the secret to Frank Jares's and Milo Steinborn's massive neck development?

"Well, I've asked them both that same question," Vic replied, "and they've both given me the same answer: 'Wrestling.'

"No sport," Vic added, "works your neck in as many directions with as much intensity as hard wrestling."

Hard wrestling, however, is not an attractive training method for most bodybuilders. Furthermore, while wrestling will certainly develop your neck, it is not the most efficient nor the safest way to work these important muscles. The efficient, safe way to build your neck is to use the Nautilus neck machines.

Nautilus Neck Machines

4-way neck: The 4-way neck is a good machine to use in a negative-emphasized manner. Basically, you'll be using your arms to assist you in doing the positive part of the movement. Transfer the weight from your hands to your neck gradually and smoothly. Lower slowly with your neck mus-

4-way neck, lateral contraction to the left: Use your left arm to assist you in doing the positive work. Lower slowly with your neck and repeat.

Rotary neck: Resist with your neck as you force your head to rotate to the right and to the left.

cles to the count of 8. Place your hands back on the movement arm and use them to help your neck do the positive portion of the exercise. Repeat the slow lowering movements for 8 to 12 repetitions. After you get the hang of this style, you'll be able to use 30 to 40 percent more resistance than you would normally handle.

Work the back of your neck first, then the front, and finally the sides.

Rotary neck: Although this machine is seldom found in commercial facilities, if you have access to it, be sure to use it. The rotary neck provides great resistance for the twisting functions of your neck. In some respects, it simulates what you might do to escape from a headlock put on you by a competitive wrestler.

To provide resistance in this machine, you must push the hand levers with your arms. The hand levers are connected to the overhead movement arm, which is padded and fits snugly around your head. Negative-only exercise can be provided by pressure on either hand lever, which will force your head to turn. This turning force is resisted by your neck muscles. Alternately perform six negative-only repetitions to the right and six negative-only repetitions to the left. Increase the intensity of the repetitions gradually, but make your last two maximum efforts.

Neck and shoulder: Shoulder shrugs for the trapezius muscles are performed on this machine. With your forearms in place and hands open, shrug your shoulders smoothly as high as possible. Do not lean back. Pause in the top position and return slowly to the bottom for a stretch. Repeat for 8 to 12 repetitions.

Lasting Strength

If you're a typical bodybuilder, you've probably never worked your neck muscles progressively. Now is the time to start. Train your neck at the end of your workout twice a week for the next month.

Your neck will quickly respond by growing larger and stronger. Continue to train your neck thereafter at least once a week. Your overall symmetry will be greatly improved.

"There's something about the fullness of a man's neck," Vic Tanny says, "that indicates confidence and toughness. And it's a true mark of lasting strength."

Start emphasizing your neck today.

Neck and shoulder: Shrug your shoulders smoothly to the contracted position, lower, and repeat.

The impressive neck of Bill Richardson.

Nautilus Neck Exercises

	Date						
4-way neck machine	Back extension						
	Front flexion						
	Right lateral contraction						
	Left lateral contraction						
	Rotary neck						
	Neck and shoulder						

Boyer Coe, Ellington Darden, and Arthur Jones answer questions at a recent Nautilus seminar in Lake Helen, Florida. *(Photos by Inge Cook)*

CHAPTER 23
QUESTIONS AND ANSWERS

No Nautilus book would be complete without a chapter on questions and answers. The following questions have been asked by bodybuilders who use Nautilus equipment.

How Muscles Grow

Q. *Is there anything new about the muscular growth process that hasn't been discussed in your previous books?*

A. The information concerning the mechanics of muscular growth in *The Nautilus Bodybuilding Book* is still valid. A brief review, however, may be helpful.

Muscles, which are involved in all human movement, exist in three basic types. The muscles used for body movement are under voluntary, conscious control. These are called skeletal muscles. The heart, automatically operated by the nervous system and not under conscious control, is composed of another kind of tissue called cardiac muscle. A third type of tissue, called smooth muscle, automatically serves internal functions, propelling food through the stomach and intestines and constricting blood vessels to adjust blood flow.

The three types of muscles are all interrelated, but only the voluntary skeletal muscles benefit directly from exercise. Cardiac muscle is strengthened by proper exercise, but this effect is secondary, as a result of increased demand on the circulatory system by the skeletal muscles.

The skeletal muscles are composed of millions of strands of a thin-filament protein called actin and a thick-filament protein called myosin. Given the presence of calcium, magnesium, and two other proteins called troponin and tropomyosin, actin and myosin can contract and move your limbs with great force.

The fuel for muscular contraction is a chemical compound called adenosine triphosphate, or ATP. When one of the three phosphates has broken off from ATP to form ADP, or adenosine diphosphate,

High-intensity exercise is one of the keys to muscular growth.

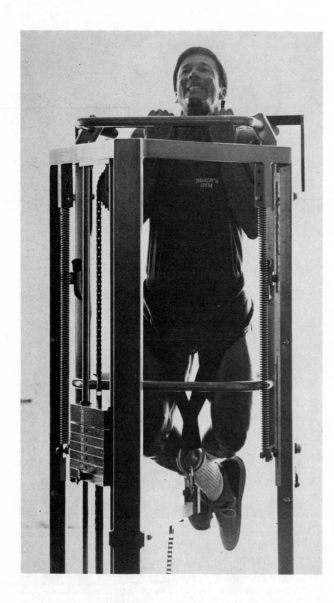

energy is released into the muscular environment. When the actin binds to myosin in the presence of calcium, the energy released from ATP breakdown is used to pull the actin filaments along the myosin filaments. More specifically, a bridge forms between actin and myosin. Energy from ATP breakdown is used to shorten the actomyosin cross-bridge, which shortens the muscle.

When a muscle is contracted repeatedly against resistance, it overcompensates by growing larger and stronger. The technical term for muscular growth is hypertrophy. The signal for hypertrophy is clearly intensity of contraction. When a muscle is faced with high-intensity requirements, it responds with a protective increase in muscular size and strength.

There are a number of physical changes seen with hypertrophy that explain increased muscular size and strength:

• The actin and particularly the myosin protein filaments increase in size.

• The number of actin/myosin units increases.

• The number of blood capillaries within the fiber may increase.

• The amount of connective tissue may increase.

In summary, when a muscle grows larger and stronger, individual muscle fibers primarily increase their volume by adding units of actin and myosin. The total number of muscle fibers, however, remains the same.

Adding ½ Inch to the Arms

Q. *Adding ½ inch to the upper arms in a week, as stated in Chapter 17, seems too good to be true. Can everyone who tries this program expect the promised results?*

A. Adding ½ inch to the upper arms in a week is what the "average" bodybuilder can expect if he follows the recommended routine. Some bodybuilders will get better gains than ½ inch and

Negative-only chins should be an important exercise in your arm-building routine.

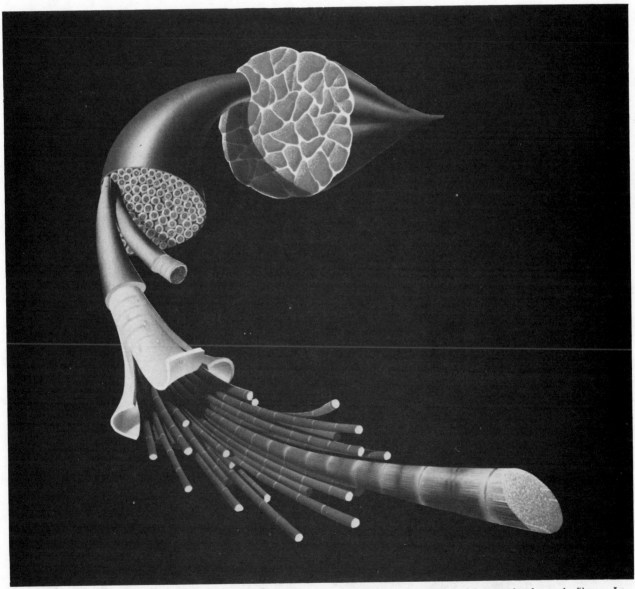

Muscles are composed of groups of separately wrapped bundles, each bundle made up of thousands of muscle fibers. A muscle fiber can be divided into myofibrils, which can be further separated into myofilaments. Myofilaments, which are composed of millions of actin and myosin units, are the primary muscle parts that increase in number as a result of high-intensity exercise. *(Drawing by Paul Hillman)*

Bertil Fox as he appeared at the 1983 Mr. Olympia contest in Munich, West Germany.

some bodybuilders will attain less than ½ inch. But the average will be approximately ½ inch on the flexed upper arm.

For example, Dana R. Lowe and Larry S. Lowe, faculty members of Loyola College of Maryland, reported on an interesting study in the August 1983 issue of *Muscle Up* magazine. They supervised the upper arm training, as described in Chapter 17, of 22 athletes. The trainees ranged in age from 15 to 42 years and their weight varied from 135 to 250 pounds.

The results of the Lowe and Lowe study were as follows: two athletes gained ⅛ inch, five gained ¼ inch, five gained ⅜ inch, three gained ½ inch, two gained ⅝ inch, two gained ¾ inch, one gained ⅞ inch, and two gained 1 inch.

The average gain on the upper arm for the 22 participants in the study was .48 inch, or slightly less than ½ inch, as a result of only three brief workouts.

The Lowes' study reinforces the experience of numerous bodybuilders who have trained at Nautilus Sports/Medical Industries in Lake Helen, Florida. Not every bodybuilder can expect to gain exactly ½ inch on his upper arms in a week. But he should expect to produce very significant improvement in the size of his biceps and triceps— and quickly.

Negative-Only Training

Q. *If negative-only training, as described in Chapter 4, is the best type of exercise, why aren't most of your advanced Nautilus routines performed in a negative-only manner?*

A. Negative-only movements, especially chins and dips on the multi-exercise machine, are incorporated in many of the advanced routines for the upper body. But as stated on the last page of Chapter 4, for best-possible bodybuilding results, negative-only exercise should be performed sparingly. Naturally, you'll want to take advantage of the muscle-stimulating effect of negative work by always performing the lowering phase of each repetition smoothly and slowly.

Q. *What's an example of a negative-only workout?*

A. Boyer Coe occasionally performs a negative-only routine for his Friday training session. The following negative-only routine was performed by Boyer on August 19, 1983:

1. Leg extension
2. Double-legged half squat
3. Leg curl
4. Calf raise
5. Lateral raise
6. Overhead press
7. Pullover
8. Decline press
9. Neck and shoulder
10. Compound position biceps
11. Abdominal

Two assistants are necessary for Boyer's negative-only workouts. The assistants must pull or push the movement arms into the contracted position; Boyer then controls the resistance and lowers it to the stretched position. The assistants do the lifting and Boyer does the lowering.

Super-Slow Training

Q. *I'm intrigued by your chapter on super-slow training. Does Boyer Coe ever train in this manner?*

A. Yes, in August of 1983, Boyer started training once a week in the super-slow fashion. It took only one super-slow workout to intrigue Boyer as well.

"I've always had trouble," Boyer says, "isolating my lats and deltoids. But with super-slow repetitions on the pullover and lateral raise, I felt I was bringing into action all possible fibers in those areas. As a result, I could feel almost immediate growth stimulation. Super-slow training also works equally well with other Nautilus machines."

Ellington Darden assists Boyer Coe in a negative-only workout.

The start of a super-slow repetition on the pullover.

The symmetrical physique of Samir Bannout, winner of the 1983 Mr. Olympia contest.

Here's a listing of Boyer Coe's super-slow routine of August 24, 1983:

1. Hip adduction
2. Calf raise
3. Neck and shoulder
4. Rowing torso
5. 70° shoulder
6. Pullover
7. 40° chest
8. Lower back
9. Chin
10. Multi biceps
11. Decline press
12. Multi triceps

Performing More Than One Advanced Routine

Q. *How many of the advanced routines can I perform in a given workout?*

A. Try to resist the temptation to perform more than two advanced routines during the same workout. For example, you might employ one of the chest and one of the arm routines on the same day. Even then, two advanced routines may leave you in a state of overtraining.

The advanced routines for the lats, chest, shoulders, thighs, calves, and arms are all designed to shock a specific muscle group into renewed growth. A specialized routine should be combined with several exercises for the other major muscles, but with the understanding that your total exercises for the workout should not exceed 12. In fact, you will probably get the best possible results if you limit your total exercises to 10 or fewer.

Remember, high-intensity Nautilus exercise *stimulates* your muscles to grow larger and stronger. But to become larger and stronger, your muscles must be *permitted* to grow. Make sure you permit your muscles to grow by not overtraining them.

Q. *What would happen if I did the advanced*

routines for the lats, chest, shoulders, thighs, calves, and arms all on the same day?

A. Trying the above routines all on the same day would, according to Arthur Jones, "kill a large male gorilla." Of course, Jones is assuming that you would perform each routine to momentary muscular failure. To accomplish such a workout, however, you would have to lessen the intensity of each routine. And lessening the intensity would mean that your muscle-building results would be slowed to a snail's pace.

The primary idea behind bodybuilding is to develop your muscles, not to see how much total exercise you can tolerate. Keep your exercise sessions intense and brief. Your body's overall recovery ability, and ultimately your muscles, will thank you for it.

Breakdown Training

Q. *I'd like to know more about the breakdown training that you recommended for the lateral raise in Chapter 13. What makes it effective?*

A. When you fail on the last repetition of the lateral raise, the reason that you have failed is not that you have zero strength. No! The reason you failed is that you have reduced your starting level of strength below the weight on the machine.

As an example, let's say a trainee can perform only 1 repetition on the lateral raise with 100 pounds. Instead of trying to perform a series of 1-repetition sets, experience shows, he will get better muscle-building results if he reduces the resistance by 20 percent and performs as many repetitions as possible. So, he puts 80 pounds of resistance on the machine. Eighty pounds feels easy at first, because he is 100 pounds strong. But with each succeeding repetition he makes a deeper inroad into his starting level of strength. On the 10th repetition, his temporary level of strength is 81 pounds. And 81 pounds of force is enough to lift 80 pounds of resistance, but just

barely. Then, the trainee fails on the 11th repetition, because 79 pounds of force will not lift 80 pounds of resistance.

Thus, 10 repetitions with 80 pounds on the lateral raise has reduced the trainee's starting level of strength from 100 pounds to 79 pounds. In doing 10 repetitions he has made a 21 percent inroad into his starting level of strength.

But what would happen if, rather than the trainee failing on the 11th repetition of the lateral raise with 80 pounds, the resistance was quickly reduced to 60 pounds? With 20 pounds less on the machine, the trainee could continue to perform repetitions until his deltoid strength was reduced below the weight on the machine. Then if the resistance was reduced from 60 to 40 pounds, he could still continue until his deltoid strength was reduced below 40 pounds.

With a normal set of 10 repetitions, a trainee reduces his starting level of strength by approximately 20 percent. By incorporating breakdowns into his routine, he has the potential to reduce his starting level of strength by 60 percent or more.

Q. *Will breakdown training stimulate my muscles to grow faster?*

A. Breakdown training can be good and bad.

It can be good because it makes a deeper inroad into your starting level of strength. Theoretically, this means that it will stimulate more muscular growth.

But it can be bad, since making a deeper inroad into your starting level of strength also makes a deeper inroad into your recovery ability. If you severely deplete your recovery ability, your muscles will not be able to overcompensate and become stronger. Too much breakdown training could actually make your body weaker rather than stronger, and your muscles smaller rather than larger.

Breakdown training is most effective when it is used on your smaller muscle groups, such as your

Three selector pins are needed for efficient breakdown training. *(Photo by Lewis Green)*

deltoids. It also works well on the biceps, triceps, and flexors and extensors of the forearms.

Do not, however, in your enthusiasm, overdo breakdown training. Keep it infrequent.

50-Repetition Calf Raises

Q. *The Nautilus guidelines suggest 8 to 12 repetitions on most exercises. In Chapter 16, why do you recommend that 50 repetitions be performed on the calf raise?*

A. Doing an exercise in an unusual manner, such as high repetitions followed by negatives, can often shock the involved muscles into renewed growth. That seems to work especially well on the calves for several reasons.

1. The gastrocnemius of the calves, because of its location, is less efficient neurologically than the muscles of the upper body. Higher repetitions, therefore, may involve more muscle fibers.

2. The range of movement of the heels in the calf raise is relatively short. Compared to a pullover, which employs a long range of movement, you can perform more repetitions in the same 60-second time frame.

3. It is convenient to perform the calf raise in a negative manner. If you grasp the overhead bars and pull with the arms, no helpers are required for the positive portion of the exercise.

It should be noted, however, that such a 50-repetition routine should *not* be performed more often than three times a week for two consecutive weeks.

Organizing Yearly Training

Q. *As an advanced bodybuilder, how should I organize my yearly training?*

A. As an advanced bodybuilder, you should be aware of your strengths and weaknesses. Your ideal should be a physique that has maximal, yet symmetrical development of all your major muscles. It makes sense, therefore, to select routines

The Nautilus side leg curl machine emphasizes the contracted position of the hamstrings. Notice that the weight stack is conveniently located in front of your hands, allowing you to do breakdowns on this machine by yourself.

A tried-and-proved way to use the duo squat machine is three times every two weeks.

that concentrate on your weaknesses. But be careful not to stay with a specialized routine for more than several weeks. You can then try another specialized routine for several more weeks. More than several weeks of an advanced routine can quickly lead to overtraining of that body part.

The majority of your yearly training, however, should be composed of basic overall-body routines. Such basic routines are listed and detailed in *The Nautilus Bodybuilding Book*.

Duo Squat Machine

Q. *How often should I use the duo squat machine in my basic routine?*

A. An excellent way to employ the duo squat machine is the method used by Boyer Coe in his February–July 1983 training.

Basically, Boyer had an A and B Workout. The A Workout began with the duo squat machine and included eight other exercises. The B Workout consisted of 11 exercises, but did not include the duo squat.

Boyer trained at 3:00 P.M. on Monday, Wednesday, and Friday of each week. He performed the A Workout, which included the duo squat machine, on Monday and Friday of one week. On Wednesday of the next week he again performed the A Workout. Boyer used the duo squat machine three times every two weeks. Eventually, after four months of such training, he reduced the use of the squat machine to once a week.

Barbell Bench Presses

Q. *I enjoy doing barbell bench presses as a part of my upper body training. How can I work them into a Nautilus program?*

A. First, you need to ask yourself what your objective is in performing the bench press. Do you perform the bench press to build your arms, your shoulders, or your chest? If so, you may be interested in the analysis below.

Powerlifters should do heavy training on the bench press no more than once a week. *(Photo by Inge Cook)*

The bench press involves several major muscle groups: the triceps, deltoids, and pectorals. But because it is a multiple-joint movement with a short range of motion, the bench press works the above major muscles through only their middle range. Thus, the bench press is a poor exercise for the triceps, deltoids, and pectorals. It does not provide anything close to full-range exercise for those important muscles.

The Nautilus double chest machine is a far better exercise for your upper body than the bench press, particularly if you are a bodybuilder.

If you are a powerlifter, however, then the bench press must be performed, since it is one of three competitive lifts. Still, as a powerlifter, you probably don't need to practice the bench press as much as you have in the past. The suggested routine would be to train no more than three times a week, say Monday, Wednesday, and Friday.

Monday would be your basic Nautilus workout: one set to failure of ten Nautilus machines. On Wednesday, you might work on the skills of powerlifting, the technical mechanics of the squat, bench press, and deadlift. No single attempts should be performed during the Wednesday workout. Friday would be your heavy repetition workout. Triples, doubles, and occasionally singles should be performed on the powerlifts. At the end of your Friday workout, you could also do a set of negative-only chins and dips.

Nutrition

Q. *Nutrition, like bodybuilding, seems to be filled with myths and superstitions. Where can I get scientific information on the importance of nutrition in bodybuilding?*

A. The field of food and nutrition indeed has its share of myths and superstitions. To help you decipher the facts from the fallacies, you should read the following books:

Vitamins and Health Foods (1981), by Victor Herbert, M.D., and Stephen Barrett, M.D. George Stickley Co., Philadelphia.

The New Nuts Among the Berries (1977), by Ronald Deutsch. Bull Publishing Co., Palo Alto, California.

The Nautilus Nutrition Book (1981), by Ellington Darden, Ph.D. Contemporary Books, Inc., Chicago.

Nutrition Concepts and Controversies (second edition, 1982), by Eva May Hamilton and Eleanor Noss Whitney, Ph.D. West Publishing Co., St. Paul, Minnesota.

Lower Back Machine

Q. *Where should the lower back machine be placed in a basic Nautilus routine?*

A. The lower back muscles, like those of the abdominal area, are directly and indirectly used to stabilize your entire body. Almost every Nautilus machine provides some work for the lower back and abdominals. Thus, the Nautilus lower back machine, as well as the abdominal machine, should be used toward the last portion of your workout.

High Repetitions for Definition

Q. *What about the idea of performing high repetitions on Nautilus machines for definition? Is there any truth to this concept?*

A. No! High repetitions for definition are a carryover from the belief that it is possible to spot-reduce fat from specific parts of the body. Spot reduction of fat is not possible.

Furthermore, performing more than 20 repetitions for a given exercise is not more effective at burning calories than using a heavier resistance and keeping the repetitions in the 8 to 12 range.

Champion Bodybuilders and Nautilus

Q. *I'm a Nautilus believer, but it still disturbs me that few champion bodybuilders use Nautilus.*

Why is that so?

A. That may have been true several years ago but today you'll find that more champion bodybuilders are using Nautilus than ever before.

It is a well-known fact that Casey Victor has used Nautilus in his bodybuilding career since 1970. Mike and Ray Mentzer have trained almost exclusively on Nautilus equipment for the last eight years. Boyer Coe has combined Nautilus with barbell training for over ten years. But since February 1983, Boyer has trained only on Nautilus.

Other champion bodybuilders incorporate various Nautilus machines into their overall workouts. Tom Platz regularly uses the Nautilus leg extension and leg curl machines. So does Bertil Fox. Frank Zane uses many of the Nautilus upper body machines, such as the double chest, 70° shoulder, multi biceps, multi triceps, and supination/pronation on the Sportsmate. Lance Dreher likes the multi biceps and multi triceps, as does Bill Grant. Kal Szkalak prefers the plate-loading biceps/triceps machine. Andreas Cahling is partial to the rowing torso and double shoulder machines. John Cardillo owns five Nautilus-equipped gyms in Canada and trains almost exclusively with the machines.

Women bodybuilders also use Nautilus. Rachel McLish likes the results she gets from the double shoulder, double chest, leg extension, and leg curl. Kiki Elomaa says that the hip abduction/adduction adds pleasing curves to her hips and thighs. Lynne Pirie keeps her torso shapely by regular use of the arm cross, lateral raise, and pullover.

Dozens of other champion bodybuilders are also finding that Nautilus produces much better results than barbells. They are proving in their own bodies what Arthur Jones said years ago, that Nautilus is the most efficient, concentrated, and productive way to build muscle.

As could be expected, however, some cham-

"Samir Bannout," says photographer Chris Lund, "has the best upper and lower back in professional bodybuilding."

pion bodybuilders do not use Nautilus. Such body-builders usually dislike Nautilus because they fail to understand the "harder-but-briefer" philosophy behind the machines. Once a trainee becomes addicted to long medium-intensity barbell work-outs, it is difficult to switch to briefer Nautilus sessions. The tendency is usually toward the "more-is-better" philosophy.

The vast majority of bodybuilders, however, are not in the champion or professional category. Many are teenagers, teenagers who can be influenced by facts rather than traditions. These young bodybuilders have not yet become addicted to marathon workouts. Their minds are open to the efficiency and productivity of bodybuilding with Nautilus.

In the future, you will see more and more begin-ning, advanced, and champion bodybuilders ad-hering to the Nautilus way, because it works.

Yes, Nautilus works. It builds muscle fast!

Rachel McLish frequently uses the Nautilus double shoulder machine.

Boyer Coe has trained exclusively on Nautilus equipment since February 1983.

CONCLUSION

Your muscles are capable of performing an enormous amount of exercise if the pace is moderate and if the intensity is low. But no amount of such exercise will produce unusual muscular size. Too much, in fact, will actually produce muscular losses.

But at the same time, it is obvious that for building muscle at least some exercise is required. So the amount can never be reduced to zero. Simple logic thus dictates the direction we should take. We should look for *the least amount of exercise that will produce the desired result.* Any exercise in excess of the minimum amount required will be wasted effort at best and counterproductive at worst.

Brief, but intense, workouts have been the cornerstone of the Nautilus philosophy since the first Nautilus machine was manufactured in 1970. The ongoing challenge to the advanced bodybuilder is the same: *brief, intense workouts.*

For bigger, stronger muscles, look for ways to make exercise briefer and more intense.

Nautilus is the logical way.

The computerized Nautilus machines of the future will make exercise even more intense.

BIBLIOGRAPHY

Darden, Ellington. *The Nautilus Book: An Illustrated Guide to Physical Fitness the Nautilus Way*, revised edition. Chicago: Contemporary Books, Inc., 1982.

————. *The Nautilus Bodybuilding Book*. Chicago: Contemporary Books, Inc., 1982.

Goldberg, Alfred L., and others. "Mechanism of Work-Induced Hypertrophy of Skeletal Muscle," *Medicine and Science in Sports* 7 (1975): 248–261.

Hutchins, Ken. "Super-Slow Protocol." Unpublished article, 1983.

Jones, Arthur. *Nautilus Training Principles, Bulletin No. 1*. DeLand, Florida: Nautilus Sports/Medical Industries, 1970.

————. *Nautilus Training Principles, Bulletin No. 2*. DeLand, Florida: Nautilus Sports/Medical Industries, 1971.

————. "The Facts Are," *Iron Man* 32, 3 (March 1973): 44, 45.

————. "The Best Kind of Exercise." *Iron Man* 32, 4 (May 1973): 36–38, 70.

————. "From Here to Infinity or Very Close, Featuring the Duo Squat Machine and Lower Back Machine," *Nautilus Magazine* 4, 6 (October/November 1982), special supplement.

————. "Exercise 1983 . . . The Possible and the Impossible, Part 3," *Nautilus Magazine* 5, 3 (June/July 1983): 97–99.

If you have questions on advanced Nautilus routines, please send a self-addressed, stamped envelope to Dr. Ellington Darden, Darden Research Corporation, P.O. Box 1016, Lake Helen, FL 32744.

Ellington Darden and Boyer Coe are available for seminars. Write to the address above for details.